John Patrick's
ADVANCED
BLACKJACK

John Patrick's
ADVANCED
BLACKJACK

John Patrick

k

Lyle Stuart
Kensington Publishing Corp.
www.kensingtonbooks.com

LYLE STUART books are published by

Kensington Publishing Corp.
850 Third Avenue
New York, NY 10022

All Kensington titles, imprints, and distributed lines are available at special quantity discounts for bulk purchases for sales promotions, premiums, fund raising, educational, or institutional use. Special book excerpts or customized printings can also be created to fit specific needs. For details, write or phone the office of the Kensington special sales manager: Kensington Publishing Corp., 850 Third Avenue, New York, NY 10022, attn: Special Sales Department, phone 1-800-221-2647.

Kensington and the K logo Reg. U.S. Pat. & TM Office
Lyle Stuart is a trademark of Kensington Publishing Corp.

First printing 1996

10 9 8 7 6 5 4 3

Printed in the United States of America

Library of Congress Cataloging-in-Publication Data
Patrick, John, 1932–
   [Advanced Blackjack]
   John Patrick's advanced blackjack / John Patrick.
      p.   cm.
   "A Lyle Stuart book."
   ISBN 0-8184-0582-1 (pbk)
   1. Blackjack (Game)   I. Title.
GV1295.B55P368   1996
795.4′2—dc20   95-47091
                                                                  CIP

To My Family:

My Mother and my father

and to my daughters Lori and Colleen.

They are my world!

PREFACE

This book covers card counting. I can take any person who plays Blackjack and teach them how to count cards. And it's a snap to learn.

The hardest part of gambling is Learning How To Win. That's because winning requires a lot of Discipline. That virtue is missing in 95% of the people who risk money in the world of gambling. If you lack Money Management and Discipline, don't feel bad—you have a lot of company.

This book will teach you how to win. It's up to you to absorb the message.

"SO YOU WANNA BE A GAMBLER!!" I'll show you how to be the best. Why be anything less?

CONTENTS

CONTENTS

Money Management

Discipline

INTRODUCTION TO GAMBLING

1

SO YOU WANNA BE A GAMBLER!

So You Wanna Be a Gambler? Do you now? Do you really know what is in store for you when you gamble? Do you realize what you are up against when you plunk a couple of dollars on a green felt and risk the chance of losing that money on the outcome of the next Blackjack hand?

There is a strong possibility you're gonna lose that money. And one of the reasons you'll probably lose is that you're a dope. You don't know how to play Blackjack.

Oh, you know the object of the game — to get as close to 21 that you can and hope the dealer has a worse hand. That is the object of the game, not the answer to how to play it.

How you play Blackjack or any other gambling outlet you may be engaged in, calls for a tedious hard boiled strong willed intelligent awareness of the entire game upon which you are risking your money.

In other words baby, you better be perfect at that particular game or don't gamble. If you decide to risk even one dollar of your hard earned money on the outcome of a hand of Blackjack, roll of the dice, spin of a Roulette wheel, decision on a ball game, or daily Lottery ticket, you are gambling and you better know what the heck you're doing.

So if you wanna get involved in gambling, you may as

well get it into your head right now: Learn everything you can about the game you attack.

In this case we're talking about Blackjack. Don't play this game until you're an expert at Basic Strategy and card counting.

I do not condone gambling by people who engage in wagering money, just for the fun of betting. I'm not trying to make you a professional gambler but I do want you to understand that this is a rough way to make money.

So You Wanna Be a Gambler!!! Then be a perfect one. Watch how your game improves.

2

A ROUGH GAME

You may as well understand what card/counting is before you jump in with both feet. Blackjack is the roughest game in the house. By far it is the toughest game for the player to win at.

Go back and read that previous paragraph 73 times.

I don't wanna hear that nonsense that has been passed down thru the years about it being the only game that can be beaten. People hear that crap, make a bee-line for the tables and get their wallets cleaned.

Blackjack is NOT the best game in the house and you better get that into your head. This is what these seers of wisdom are trying to say: "Blackjack is the only game where the player has an opportunity to get an edge on the house."

But people only hear the first part of that statement and think Blackjack is the game to play. NO, no, no, a thousand times no.

What is meant — but never explained — is that when you are an experienced card counter, you have an edge on the house of approximately 2%. Now that in itself is good but how many people are bona fide card counters?

It is estimated that only one out of every 100,000 Blackjack players are truly proficient card counters and that is a crime, since it is so easy to become one.

But that still leaves about 99,999 players out of 100,000 that do not have that 2% edge and they are the ones who are getting whacked.

At every lecture I give, in every class, or in every discussion on gambling, I come out and say: "Don't play Blackjack." And the reason is because most people are too stubborn to learn how to count.

If you follow everything I lay out on these pages and conscientiously practice a couple of hours a week, you will find out how easy it is. And you will become a perfect player. Then, and only then, should you play Blackjack.

3

BIG 4

Stop right where you are. If you have ever read any of my books, you'll know exactly what I'm gonna say in this chapter — and it won't hurt you to read it again. The items listed will provide all you need to win at gambling. Of course you gotta have the intestinal fortitude to follow every step, but there is no question that here is the key to winning.

The front cover spells it out for you and each part of this book dedicates a section for each of the 4 things you need to win: It's called the Big Four:

1) BANKROLL
2) KNOWLEDGE OF THE GAME
3) MONEY MANAGEMENT
4) DISCIPLINE

This is the whole secret to gambling, regardless of what you play. If more people would realize this and curtail their gambling forays until they had these four items, it would change the whole world of gambling as we now know it.

Guys like Imus Bettmore would control his ridiculous charge into a casino and wager within the confines of his own individual Bankroll. But this unthinking idiot, just like the thousands of people like him, gambles — just for the sheer pleasure of 'taking a risk.'

They think that the excuses they give: 'gambling for

fun' condones the fact that they can throw money into games that will eventually wipe them out and for no other reason than they lack one, two, three or all parts of the Big 4.

If you feel I'm talking directly to you, then maybe I am. And if you think it makes me feel bad that I might be hurting your feelings, then put that thought out of your mind. I see stupid jerks at the tables every day, making ridiculous bets and moves, and it honestly gets to me. So if I've touched a tender spot, that's your problem. My intention is to make you aware of what a boob you are and maybe correct this illogical approach to gambling.

1) **BANKROLL:** This is your own individual decision and is based strictly on the amount you set aside on a given day or week. If you plan a trip to the casinos and bring $300. with you — then every single decision you make that day, as to planned profits and losses, is based on that $300. A dope like Imus Bettmore cannot bet any more than what will be laid out for him. And if that disappoints him and restricts his so-called plans to let it all hang out...than his problems are a lot deeper than what I can do for him. Bankroll is the beginning and sets up every monetary move you make. If you don't have the proper Bankroll, you can't and shouldn't gamble — period. Wait until you have the proper bread — the tables will still be there.

2) **KNOWLEDGE OF THE GAME:** You gotta be perfect baby, not just good or pretty good or very good, I mean absolutely perfect in your knowledge of the game you attack.

G. Ahsgood thinks he is a good blackjack player. He's been to every casino in the civilized world and has played blackjack for 57 years. He can pronounce blackjack in 14 different languages, spell it backwards, and name the 3 children of the guy it was named after. He also stands with a hard 15 vs. the dealers ace. He's a dope. Knowing the object of the game doesn't mean diddedly dang.

You could plop a 3-year-old cross-eyed urangatan at a blackjack table, deal him a series of hands and have his blinking key the decision as to whether he will hit or stand. Maybe he'll win 7 out of 10 hands. Does that make him an expert player? No way!

You gotta be absolutely perfect in your knowledge of the game you play, and even that will bring you to only a little less than a 50-50 chance of winning a hand.

The way I see people at these tables, I think sometimes I'd pick the urangatan to be my partner in a blackjack tournament. And that ain't just monkey jive.

3) **MONEY MANAGEMENT:** You gotta know every bet you will make following a loss and every bet you will make following a win. This part of gambling usually is the downfall of the majority of players. Mr. Gess Watt loves to play blackjack. He knows basic strategy, but when it comes to making his wagers, it's anybody's guess what Gess Watt will bet. His decisions are strictly guess work as to how he 'feels' he will do on each hand and has no planned pattern. He could play for an hour, win 32 hands, lose 13 and end up being out $250. Lack of Money Management. Guess what Watt will do! He'll blame everybody in the casino except himself. Money Management is the key to winning and the thing I stress in later chapters.

4) **DISCIPLINE:** The ball game!!! The whole answer to winning. Guts! It is by far the most important part of gambling. All of the other parts of the Big 4 are needed in order to compete intelligently, but the one thing that is hardest to acquire and to hold on to, is DISCIPLINE. It is what separates the novice from the professional. Discipline!!!

Get it — or get out of gambling. Later chapters will spell this out in detail and it behooves you to hang on every word.

There you have the Big 4. Each of the upcoming Sections will be dedicated to one particular part of the Big 4 and will contain it's own set of separate chapters. When you are finished, and understand the need for the Big 4 — your job will be to get them and master them.

You will become a perfect player. Your losing days will not be totally devastating and your winning days will come more often, because you'll be accepting lesser amounts but getting them more often.

Am I getting your attention?

4

LITTLE THREE

In order of importance, this set of three items ranks behind the Big 4, but in their own way have a direct bearing on putting together a whole new outlook on gambling.

Forget all the garbage that has been handed down through the years about the world of wagering:

a) Gamblers always die broke,
b) Always split aces and eights,
c) Gamble only for fun,
d) The game is rigged,
e) The Roulette wheel is gaffed,
f) The deck is marked,
g) The dice are loaded,
h) The quarterback is on the take,
i) The fix is on,
j) The fighter with the black trunks is in the tank,
k) The 'boys' got to the jockey,
l) The house never loses,

I'm sure you've heard some or all of the above at one time or another. And *if* you have and *if* you believe any of them, then why be such a boob and still gamble?

I don't wanna waste time breaking all of these sayings down, but the quotes are usually bellowed by losers, or people who know nothing about gambling (Which, by the way, could encompass about 95% of the people who gamble anyway. But that's another story.).

Take for instance the gaffed Roulette wheel. It would take you a year of Tuesdays to chart every wheel, to even get an inkling that something is up. And thousands of people who lose at the track swear that the jockey was dragging his heels trying to slow down his mount. Stop your bellyaching and concentrate on how to attack the games overall, instead of crying in your beer every time things don't go your way.

There are shady things that have happened, is happening, and will continue to happen as long as human beings have some type of control. But overall the games are straight up.

If you play in a weekly poker game where you think somebody is dealing with tricky fingers you have a variety of options:

    a) Catch him in the act and break his arm,
    b) Confront him eyeball to eyeball,
    c) Quit the game
    d) Stop your whinning, (maybe you're just a rotten player)

But stop looking for excuses for losing. Most losses can be attributed directly to a lack of the Big 4, so check and see if you have all of those things. Just wipe all of that nonsense out of your head and adopt a new approach. Let's go to the Little 3.

    1) THEORY
    2) LOGIC
    3) TRENDS

1) **THEORY:** I've been gambling since the Big Apple of New York was a little seed and have had more than my share of bad days and good days. The hurt on those losing days rarely made up for the winning ones and yet I thought

I knew about the games. I read every book put out and still got belted too often to mention. It was time for a change. I came up with my own "THEORY" as to how to gamble.

After you read about my approach, conservative as it is, you'll come up with your own theory or approach. This will be your opinion as to how to win. That's what I want you to have; a strong theory as to how to play.

Maybe you'll like mine or maybe you'll deviate and come up with a different view. I don't give a rat's tail whether you play conservative or aggressive — just as long as you play intelligently and win consistently.

Theory — it's an opinion as to how to attack a problem. Develop one that you are comfortable with and stick to it.

2) **LOGIC:** Ken Eyefite loses his girl to an all-state football player and wants to fight the guy to save his ego. Chances are Ken Eyefite will find out he can't. A more logical move would be to find another girl. But logic and love never seem to mix. And neither does logic and gambling.

If you would take a logical approach to each facet of wagering, you'd see how the more intelligent move will turn out to be the most beneficial one.

Let's take a quick example with a football game. Ima Fan is a big booster of the Rhode Island Rosettes and bets that they beat the Buffalo Bullys in the upcoming grudge match. The Rosettes are 0-8 and haven't scored a touchdown in 4 years. The Bullys haven't lost in seven years and have set a worlds record of breaking the legs of at least 9 players in each of their last 17 games.

Ima Fan is betting on the Rosettes strictly because he likes them and not for any other reason. The logical move would be to bet with his head — not his heart. And so he continues to lose.

Many players are victims of this illogical approach to gambling. If they would sit back, analyze their play and bet only when the move makes the most sense, a whole new horizon would appear. But alas and alack, the gambling casinos are filled with players who will not apply logic to their play or their betting. So, the house continues to win. I want you to take a logical approach to whatever game you decide to concentrate on.

3) **TRENDS:** This is the third and most important part of the Little 3. This part of gambling should probably be added to the Big 4 since it is so important. Throughout the book, you will see me allude to trends.

In fact, to emphasize my feeling on TRENDS, you'll find the entire next chapter applies completely to this area.

There you have the Little 3. Keep them in mind as you put together your attack plan. Each offers a strong element of input into the minimizing of losses. And that's a major point in your learning process.

5

TRENDS

Trends, streaks, patterns — I don't give a ding what you call them. Just remember that they are a fantastically powerful force in the world of gambling and handicapping the games you might play.

In fact, I know of guys who've been wagering for years, flash a blank stare as soon as I start talking to them about streaks. Most of them operate under the same antiquated assumption that when something happens, then the opposite is due to occur. No! No! A billion times, No!!!

My theory (and in case you've already forgotten, we covered Theory just one chapter ago) is that if you catch a hot trend in any form of gambling, you ride that wave until it breaks. Yet you can stand at a craps table and watch the wildmen of the world constantly fighting the trends and attempting to outguess the dice, by making bets on situations that they 'feel' will happen, or is 'due' to happen or 'should' happen.

Most of these guys operate under the same mistaken idea that if 4 passes in a row occur, then the odds are in favor of a losing roll popping out. This is just not so. I want you to follow whichever way the pattern at a particular table may be heading. I strongly suggest you give a second look to this method of play.

To make my point, let's start with the flipping of a coin. It doesn't matter the total number of flips, that's up to you. Make it 200 - 300 - 400 whatever you want. Be sure and record the outcome, in order, on a sheet of paper.

When you're finished, it will not matter which is the highest total — heads or tails, although chances are the results should be pretty close.

Now go back and look over the chart you made of those 300 flips. Take notice of how many streaks have shown. It won't be a constant reading of head, tail, head, tail, head, etc. You will find 2 - 3 - 4 - 5 - 6 of one or the other appearing on numerous occasions.

Even though the chances of head or tail showing is strictly 50-50, you'll find that streaks will always prevail.

This is true in Roulette, where the color black may show five times in a row and then red for seven in a row. Or in sports, the Yankees could win 8 games in a row and then go into a slump and lose 4 in a row. Who can explain it? Nobody, cause it happens so often and in every game you will play.

Suppose the Yanks did win 8 games in a row, which is not unlikely. Eyeam Dubblin has a theory that when a team wins 3 games in a row, then he jumps in and starts doubling his bet that they will lose a game. Can you imagine this poor Dubblin bumpkin watching 3 wins occur and then start doubling up that they will lose?

The next five wins will, or at least should, put an end to that ridiculous thinking cause those next five wins will bury him. More people go broke with this type of thinking then you may imagine. Think of it now. Are you one of those characters?

Nobody can explain why these streaks occur, but I base most of my handicapping in sports or charting tables in a casino, on the way the trend is going. When that particular trend starts to change, I either 'follow the trend' or leave that table and find a game that is going in the direction I have pre-determined to follow.

Let's give an example with the simple game of Roulette and go with the outside bet of Black/Red.

Since I believe so strongly in trends, I look for a streak to start. I decide on the color Black and walk over to a table. Suppose the number 3 came up on the next spin. Three is red, so no wager is made. Next spin shows 19. Again it was red and again no wager.

Bang — up pops number 10 black. I then bet on black for the next spin. Sure, I give up the first hit, but if black starts to show, I'm right there with a strong Money Management method, which we'll get into later.

The idea is this: I'll catch every streak of black that shows on the table. Suppose 4 blacks appear in a row and then red rears it's ugly head. My streak is over and no bet is made on the upcoming spin. Naturally a chopping pattern can beat me, but I will only get beaten 3 or 4 spins and bango, that session is closed and I simply leave that table.

Don't discount trends in gambling. Always look for the game of your choice to be showing a strong pattern toward one side. Then jump right in and ride that streak.

Since we're talking Blackjack and card counting, naturally there'll be chapters showing you how to find these hot or cold dealers and how to utilize those patterns. Personally, I pre-determine how I want to bet and then keep looking until a particular table is going the way I want to play.

This usually takes a lot of time, looking to find the proper streak, but the monetary return eventually will cure your tender case of "lackofactionitis."

TRENDS: a dominant part of gambling and a big, big factor in determining winning sessions.

6

WHAT IS BLACKJACK?

You want my opinion on Blackjack? It's the roughest game in the casino, bar none. Because of all of the decisions that must be made, this is the game that calls for the most amount of knowledge. And knowledge has always been a lacking ingredient in the heads of many so-called gamblers.

When Las Vegas opened back in the 1940's. Blackjack was the most popular game in the house and it still is. The reason for that is the illogical feeling among gamblers that they know how to play Blackjack.

No they don't!!! They only know the object of the game and this is the 2nd time in 10 minutes I've told you that. I want you to hang on that explanation so you don't go getting carried away by the thought, that after you memorize a basic strategy chart, you're ready to enter the worlds championship of professional Blackjack players! You ain't.

As the years passed after Vegas opened, mathematical geniuses like John Scarne and Julian Braun studied the game of Blackjack and discovered when to stand, or hit or double or split, based on which decision would cause the least number of losses — in the long run.

These men, in my mind, paved the way for serious players to intelligently tackle the game. They were not gamblers, but their findings opened up a whole new world to men who could take their findings and apply advanced theories of logic, to give the player a decent shot at the tables.

The casinos, acknowledging that these studies were making cuts into their profits, increased the amount of decks in a game to two.

This caused only a temporary set-back to the analysts, who now knew they were on the right track, and proceeded to step up their studies.

In the early sixties, the words card/counting first made significant impact. Books were written explaining how the knowledge of card counting would make instant winners of every player.

Through the 70's some strong pros mastered the game, and the casinos, in an effort to thwart these strong players, increased the amount of decks in a shoe to 4, then to 6 and finally to 8.

The popularity of the game of Blackjack gained in momentum, due to the tremendous amount of publicity it was receiving. People would read the stories about the casinos barring card counters and immediately the idea reached these players that blackjack was the game to play.

Did these boobs learn how to card count? No way! They figured their own basic knowledge of the game was enough to carry them through. They poured to the tables and they got whacked, and they're still getting whacked.

Now let's go back to my original question — What is Blackjack? Again I repeat: It is the roughest game in the casino, because of all the decisions that must be perfected.

As we go deeper into this study of card counting, I want you to thoroughly understand that if you are gonna play this game, then realize how tough it is and what you shoud have in order to compete:

    a) An intelligent pre-determined **theoretical** idea of how to approach the game,

    b) A **logical** application of all of the rules of basic

strategy,

c) A determination to look for, and follow, the **trends** of each separate shoe,

d) A decent **Bankroll** to stay in the game,

e) An absolute complete **Knowledge** of every part of the game,

f) A strong **Money Management** method,

g) And an almost fanatical application of the **Discipline** it takes to win.

My, my, my. Doesn't that seem like a condensed version of the Little 3 and Big 4!!! And yet that is all it takes to play this game successfully.

So throw away all those pre-historic notions and ideas that you had about blackjack. Realize that the hype about it being the best game in the house is a lot of hog wash. It is only good for you if you're a perfect player. That's what I'll try to make you, by getting you to be a strong card counter.

BANKROLL

7

THE FIRST STEP

If you ain't got wings you can't fly. So, if you have no bread you can't gamble. But let's look and see what people do in these two instances.

First off, they accept the fact that they don't have wings, so they put it out of their minds about sailing off into the blue.

But a guy struggling to make rent payments, car payments, college payments, food bills, hospital and insurance bills, and all the rest of the necessary evils in life, makes four bets a week on football games, figuring maybe he'll win and pick up a couple of bucks. He loses and now he's gotta get up the money for the local bookie.

Or he'll go to a casino with the hundred dollars he was gonna use for his car payment and blow it playing blackjack, a game in which he has no concept of — at all.

This is not an uncommon habit among people in general and you in particular. You're always thinking you can get hot or lucky or whatever you call it and pick up the left wing of the casino. It just doesn't happen that way.

Bankroll is the first part of the Big 4 and the stepping stone for your gambling forays. I realize Money Management and Discipline are the keys to winning, but don't discount the importance of the Bankroll. It dictates every bet you make, what your Win Goals for the day are, and what your Loss Limits should be. Bankroll sets the stage and every decision reflects back to the amount of money that you started with.

You can look it up in the dictionary — Bankroll does not mean thousands of dollars needed to gamble. The amount that each individual takes to the casino, is his own individual starting cache, and all monetary decisions are automatically based on that amount.

You do NOT dictate how much you want to win that day. It's already going to be decided by the size of your Bankroll.

If you take $300 or $200 or even $100 with you — then that's your Bankroll, however small you may think it is.

As we go deeper into the games, you'll see where there are amounts I want you to take with you to the table. A bad point is that the minimums are $5, $10, $25 and up in the Atlantic City casinos. In Vegas there are $2 and $1 tables and that gives the player a good chance to develop a winning trend. Eventually Atlantic City will get the smaller minimums and that should make it a great game for everyone to compete at.

Just remember this, Bankroll is the beginning and you should not gamble until you can do so with the proper amount of money. Regardless of what you want to do!

8

TABLE MINIMUMS

Ah...here's the big, big drawback for the average player in a casino. It is a rule set by the house, that establishes the smallest amount that a person can wager on a hand of Blackjack, or roll of the dice, or spin of a Roulette wheel.

It's there for a purpose and a very effective one at that. First of all, you must realize that most people, and I mean 90% of the people who go into the casino, play with short Bankrolls. In a later chapter I'll set up the amounts you should have and you'll see if you are among that 90%. For now let's look at the ulterior motive behind the words: 'minimum bet.'

You all understand what 'maximum bet'.means. Usually at a $5 minimum table they put a maximum of $500 that can be bet on a single hand. But that is just to protect themselves against a super high roller, who'll use a type of Martingale doubling up method, that could take all controls away from the house.

But the high roller can always get the maximums waived, so there's no point in discussing that facet of play, as most people won't get to the point where the maximum rule becomes a factor.

But that minimum can become quite a problem. The casinos, well aware of the fact that people come with small amounts, impose this minimum bet, to insure against someone 'tying' up a seat for long periods of time.

Usually in Vegas there are many $1 and $2 tables where a guy with a handful of one dollar chips can last a long long time. It doesn't matter to them, because there are so many casinos and so many tables, that they're happy for the action.

In Atlantic City there is usually a crying need for seats, so the weekends and summertime allow the casinos to impose this minimum and keep raising it.

You've probably seen the minimums at a particular table start at $3, jump to $5 around noon, to $10 at 2 PM, and $25 at five o'clock, based on the need for seats.

And sure enough a lot of people will fall right in line, playing at tables that are way out of their Bankroll range.

Shorty Shortchange enters the casino with a $150 Bankroll, plops down at a $10 table because that's the only one with an empty seat and starts to play. This sap slips his paper boy a quarter tip at Christmas and then acts like betting $10 a hand is something he does regularly.

His guts are churning as he loses 2 straight bets at $10 a pop. He is positively operating with a scared Bankroll and is petrified that his whole wad could be gone in 30 minutes and he'll have no money to play with over the next few hours.

Right off the bat he starts looking for ways to make the money last. He is dealt an eleven against the dealers up card of 5, which is a move that cries out for a double down wager.

But Shorty Shortchange is running short of capital and allows his small stack of chips to determine his Knowledge moves. Realizing he should double his bet by sliding another $10 chip onto the lay-out, he reverts to 'scared tactics' and just calls for a hit. The hand is completed and the dealer busts. Instead of winning $20, he wins $10 and now he starts cursing himself out for blowing the chance to pick up some profit.

He decides to try and skip a hand, so he drops his watch on the floor as the dealer is prepared to come out with the next hand. Ah ha — the trick works. The dealer passes him by and Shorty doesn't have to make the ten dollar bet.

But Sappy Shorty Shortchange just hit into a double play. As he fumbles to complete his charade, the dealer busts again and he is out the money he would have won that time.

Then, as he reaches down to retrieve his watch, he gasps in horror. The 250 lb. guy in the next seat picks that instant to slide off his stool and wouldn't you know — his foot lands squarely on Sidneys $75 gold watch!!! All that remains is the leather band.

Before the shock wave dies down, the dealer grumbles to Shorty: "Sir, if you're gonna sit at this table you gotta bet every hand!"

You think this is a far fetched story? I've seen guys spill drinks on themselves to avoid having to make a bet on a hand but still want to retain their seats.

It is scared money at high minimum tables and the Shorty Shortchanges of the world haven't got the money to compete intelligently, nor the guts to back off when they're over matched.

I don't blame the casinos. As long as people flock to the tables with their scared and short Bankrolls, the casinos will set the limits and minimums as they see fit.

A five dollar minimum bet is too high for a player with a $200 Bankroll. You could play at a $1 or $2 table with this amount, but not at a $5 table. If you won't buy this advice — that's your problem — but you better get one thing into your stubborn heads: "Minimums will kill you."

There is a definite reason why these minimums are set

and I've told you why, other than the fact that the casinos like you. If you still think you can play at a $5 table with a $50 buy-in — go ahead.

And when they clean you out, give me a call. I've got a uranium mine in my backyard that'll kick off 80 million dollars a year and I'll let you have it cheap, for only $100...cause I like you!!!

9

SCARED MONEY

Actually, this ties in with the previous chapter on table minimums, but I want to elaborate on just what scared money is.

Millions of people bet every day — more than you can imagine — and most bet with money they can ill afford to lose. And that's another point I want to get to.

Four hundred and sixty three times a month, someone will tell me they take an amount of money to the casinos that they 'can afford to lose.' My answer to them is always in the same vein, except the words might become rearranged to coincide with my anger at that silly statement:

    a) "Then you're a jerk..."
    b) "Well, you're a fool..."
    c) "You're a stinking liar..."

Those are three of the nicer answers I give them. Can you imagine a rather intelligent man of 35, holding down a good job in the insurance business, raising four kids, supporting a nice wife, being an upstanding church-going community conscious individual and wanting me to buy that crap that he can "afford to lose $300." It's a ridiculous statement by an otherwise rational individual.

No, he can't afford to lose $300. He just tries to con himself into thinking it doesn't bother him, cause he doesn't want it to weigh heavily on his mind as he heads home from the casino — broke!

25

He tries to shove it into the category of 'pin money' or 'excitement money' or 'entertainment expenses,' but the bottom line is that he is too stupid to know how to play intelligently and then sets out to condone his silly approach by offering childish excuses.

The same is true for the person who goes to a casino with $50 or $100 to compete and jumps up to a $5 table or dollar slot machine. He is going with too short a Bankroll. I'm not telling you to bring the family jewels, but I am telling you to stop going with that small Bankroll or scared money.

You think by taking only $100 with you, restricts your losses. What it does is prevent you from having a decent chance to get a trend in your favor. All of this will be elaborated upon in later chapters, but I want you to face gambling with an intelligent outlook and playing with scared money is not the way to begin your day.

The less you bring, the more scared you will play. I am going to give you goals to shoot for, based on your starting Bankroll. If you're starting with short amounts, you'll only be reducing your chances of staying alive at a table until a streak shows in your favor.

Think of how many times you uttered these silly works to yourself: "I'll bring down an amount I can afford to lose."

You can't afford to lose spit, so be prepared to gamble only when you're financially heeled, as well as being knowledgeably equipped.

Don't become one of the Shorty Shortchanges of the world. Give yourself a decent shot at picking up consistent returns.

10

NEED

You'll find yourself in this chapter, so don't try to point a finger at your neighbor as to who I am gearing these words at.

"Why do people gamble?" Good question, and it is my humble opinion that they gamble out of NEED! I didn't say greed — I said NEED! It is this need that drives most people to risk money to make money. Let's list some of these needs...

a) You NEED money,
b) You NEED the excitement,
c) You NEED the outlet from your daily routine,
d) You NEED the aura of casino life to build your fantasies,
e) You NEED to be part of the casino crowd,
f) You NEED to compete at the tables, to have action,
g) You NEED to show yourself that you can win,
h) You NEED to con yourself into the fact that the money you win will give your family those little 'extra things,'
i) You NEED to have something going for you each day,
j) My opinion is you NEED to have your head examined if your NEED is more than one of the above.

I disagree with all of the above (except j), unless you're

a perfect player. The object of gambling is to take the Knowledge, add the other parts of the Big 4, and go to the casinos to grind out a logical return.

You wanna gamble? Go ahead, but have the Big 4 and at least admit to yourself why you gamble. Having an 'outlet from your daily routine' is not an intelligent excuse.

I think most people gamble for need of money and need for excitement. But the thrill of anticipation quickly wears off as you start to lose money. Gambling for the thrill of it, is surely an expensive way to get your jollies. I do not condone that excuse, or most of the others I listed.

Now we get to 'Need for Money.' Many players try to hide behind the other excuses, but basically it is this 'need for money' that drives the people to gamble on sports, Blackjack, Craps, Baccarat, Roulette, Poker, Bingo, Lottery, anything. And most people won't admit it.

Hey man, if that's your reason for gambling so be it. There's nothing wrong with gambling for money cause you need it, but there is something wrong if you gamble for money and don't know how to win.

Ineeda Scorr is in a little money bind. She has been saving nickels and dimes for five years and has managed to hide away about $600. She wants to take a strong pop at the tables.

Through the years she has mastered the game of Blackjack and become a proficient card counter. She has decided to take the $600 and attack the tables. She figures $300 will help her out and swears she'll quit as soon as she reaches that amount.

Armed with her proficient Knowledge of Blackjack, a $600 Bankroll, and trusty Rosary Beads, Ineeda Scorr sets out to make her score.

Bang!!! First table she catches a cold dealer and inside

of two hours is $340 to the good. Bye-bye time has arrived. But not for Ineeda. Ineeda's need has been satisfied, now the ugly element of greed has taken over.

She figures this is her day and she may as well go for the kill. You've heard the story 700 times and probably lived it another 700 times. Before she squirms off her stool, Ineeda Scorr needs an aspirin. Her head is splitting.

She blew not only the $340 winnings, but the $600 Bankroll. In fact, before she left the table, she sold her gold lighter for $7, her class ring for $2, her scarf for $1, and her phone number for $7.50.

Another case where need brought her to the table and once that need was satisfied, she reverted to a rotten disciplined pawn.

If you've suffered through one or more of these situations don't feel bad — you have a lot of company.

Need brings a lot of people to the tables, and greed brings a lot of people to their knees. In my opinion, NEED is the driving force behind why people gamble.

And once that need is satisfied, don't be like the Ineeda Scorr's of the world. You don't need to become a permanent part of that chair. Get in your car and scoot with the loot. And yes — that's very tough to do.

11

YOUR BANKROLL

I've already told you that each person is responsible for his or her own personal Bankroll, but there are amounts that you honestly should adhere to and these amounts will be attuned to the table minimums.

To gamble at a Blackjack table, you should have 30 times the amount of the minimum at that table. This will allow you to play comfortably, waiting for the 'trend' to appear. You gotta give that 'trend' a chance to show. So running up to a table, buying in for $20, and making three or four bets doesn't allow a definite pattern to appear.

Following is the amount you should bring to a table:

    a) Three dollar table. . .30 times the amount $90
    b) Five dollar table . . . . 30 times the amount $150
    c) Ten dollar table . . . . 30 times the amount $300
    d) Twenty five dollar
       table . . . . 30 times the amount . . . $750
    e) $100 table . . . . 30 times the amount . . $3000

Now, you're not gonna lose that amount, because you'll have Win Goals and Loss Limits to protect you, but this is the amount you should bring to that game.

Looking back over that chart, how many of you have gone up to a table with less than the prescribed amount? I'd say about 90% of you are guilty of playing short.

How many of you have sidled up to a $10 Blackjack game and bought in for $50? Be honest! Can you imagine the difference between playing with $50 and playing with

$300? You lose two bets with a $50 stake and the sweat pours from your pores until your poor little brain starts searching for excuses for you to leave the table.

Aha! You have the reason! You glance at your watch and then exclaim loud enough for everyone at the table to hear you! "Wow, look at the time — I gotta run." As if anybody cared!!

You slide off the stool and go off in a corner to pout and curse out the guy who invented Blackjack in the first place.

Don't put yourself into this position with short or scared Bankrolls at high minimum tables or haven't you read the past couple of chapters? Take a glance back at the amount you need at each table and don't play until you have that amount.

12

SESSIONS

OK, you know how much you should bring to a table, so we'll now go into how you handle the Bankroll that you bring to a casino.

Since I am such a strong believer in Trends, it is only natural that the thing to do is stay alive at the table until you get involved in a hot streak.

And the way to guarantee that you don't drop your whole Bankroll at the first table, is to get you to divide it into Sessions. You will break that Bankroll into equal amounts, so that you can play at no less than three different tables, or sessions.

In this way you get three shots at the casino and in all probability, one of those Sessions should give you a hot run. Again I tell you that future chapters will cover your Win Goals and Loss Limits at each Session, but for now get to understand the reason for dividing your money into thirds.

The hardest part of winning for anybody, is getting into the habit of walking away from a table when you're losing, and also quitting when you get ahead.

The Sessions breakdown takes care of all of that. Whatever you bring to the casino is your Bankroll. First thing you do is break that money into 3 equal amounts. Each third will be brought to a different table, to begin a new Session.

Following is how you would make these splits:

BANKROLL	PER SESSION	TABLE MINIMUM
$300	$100	$3
$450	$150	$5
$600	$200	$5
$750	$250	$5
$900	$300	$10
$1000	$335	$10
$1200	$400	$10
$2250	$750	$25
$100	$35	Stay Home

Take a look at the last two figures. You go short and you go looking for trouble. Better you don't go and how many of you cats play at a $25 table with less than the required $750?

Oh, I know you could play with $600 or $500, but now you're looking to break some rules — or at least bend them! And I'm trying to instill strict discipline habits.

So if you have a Bankroll of $1800, get your butt down to the $10 tables. Maybe that's a blow to your ego, but I'm interested in protecting blows to your pocketbook.

This way you've got chips to play very comfortably and there's always the option of increasing your bets, when you slide into a nice winning streak.

You know, it's not written in stone that you break your Bankroll into three sessions, but I realize that most people go with sort of strained amounts. So my suggestions have always been to break your money into 3 tables or sessions.

However, let's say you bring $600 to the casino and don't wish to play at three sessions of $200 each. You could go to four sessions with $150 per session and still be within the suggested guidelines.

A $900 Bankroll could be broken into six separate sessions and so on. You get the point.

Already, sixty four people are writing me letters asking why they can't go to a table with 20 times the minimum, or 25 times, or 15 times. Well, save your stamps, cause I'll try to answer you.

I picked 40 times the minimum a long time ago and maintained that amount. Recently I reduced it to 30 times the minimum, in order to reach more people who come to my classes. A lot of them couldn't bring 40 times the minimum.

Now you are thinking in terms of dropping that amount to 20 times or 15 times.

Hold it! Hold it! Stop looking for ways to bang holes into strong disciplined approaches. I adhere to the 30 times per minimum and pass that suggestion over to you.

You wanna listen, good!! You wanna set your own session amounts, that's your decision and your theory, and theory is never wrong — when you're a perfect player.

You know where I stand — 30 times the table minimum. Period!!!

13

THE SERIES

The next step in breaking down your Bankroll is the Series. No problem understanding it's meaning, as it's very simple. The Series begins with the first bet you make at a Session and continues as long as that Series of bets kicks off wins.

As soon as you lose, that Series is over and the next bet begins a new Series. Future chapters in the Money Management section explain how you will bet in a Series, but for now I want only to explain it's meaning.

Of course, the betting method of what to bet when you win, and what to bet when you lose is the key to utilizing streaks, but we'll get to that in due time. Just keep your pants on. I like to do things in order.

An important point I'd like to make, is how you position your Series wins in relation to the stack of chips in front of you. Let's go back to square one.

a) You take $600 to the casino — it's your Bankroll,

b) You break the $600 into Sessions — $200 per Session,

c) Walk up to a table (session) with $200 and buy in,

d) Dealer gives you $200 in chips and you stack them in a pile in front of you

e) Slide your first bet onto the lay-out — a series has begun, (say $8 bet)

f) Assume you win $8. Instead of pulling your profit back to your session pile, start another pile in between your Series bet and and your Session pile.

35

Now, I'll explain why I want you to do this. Psychologically you will put yourself in an 'up' pattern. If you bring the profit from the first win back to that 'profit pile' and then lose the bet that is still out there — you accomplish something.

Even though your bet went down, you now have chips to pull back to your Session money, before you lay out chips for the start of a new Series.

Sometimes a Series streak will have quite a few chips in that profit pile and you feel good, knowing that even when you lose, you got a nice piece of change coming to you. It's a little thing, but the casino uses psychological tools, so you might as well do the same.

They do it with low lights, beautiful surroundings, soft music, cocktail waitresses in alluring outfits — or hadn't you noticed the girls, you sly dog!

I know some guys who can rattle off the exact measurements of every girl on each shift in his favorite casino, but needs a dealer to tell him what his Blackjack hand total is when he's dealt a two, three, five and seven. But then he becomes a mathematical computer where one of the waitresses numbers are concerned.

That's hype they're wearing, baby, and it works. So you use hype back again, even if it's just to build up your confidence.

Incidentally, if you lose the first 4 hands at a table — that Session is over and you move on. No excuses.

Four straight losses at the beginning of a Session is enough to signal you that this ain't your table — so push on. And it doesn't matter that the other tables are full, or you've ordered a drink, or the dealer is easy to talk with, or any other silly excuses.

Four initial losses mean you can't even get a Series

started. You'll find fertile ground at another game.

That's the pattern for handling your money, so remember it:

1) BANKROLL
2) SESSIONS
3) SERIES

The Series continues until a loss occurs. When that loss pops up, take back any money that may be in that middle or profit pile and bring it back to the Session amount. Then take the chips that you will use to start another series and make your bet. There's a little hype in there to keep you thinking and feeling good, but it's for a purpose.

14

MINIMIZING LOSSES

This chapter won't take long cause it's message is pure and simple.

My entire approach to gambling is very clear. The object of my theory is to Minimize Losses.

I try to keep your losses to a minimum, by holding your bets down and keeping you in the game as long as possible — until that inevitable hot streak shows.

At one of the Sessions you should catch that streak. But you gotta have money to compete. If your Bankroll is gone, the hottest streak in gambling history couldn't help you, if you're not at the table to be able to bet.

My entire approach is geared to keeping your losses to the barest minimum and while you may not like it, the results will eventually win you over to that type of thinking.

Bern N. Whole has $300 and it's burning a hole in his pocket. He can't wait to get into action.

Three minutes after he reaches the casino, he's betting $50 a roll at craps, itching to bet $100. He catches a cold streak and drops his wad in 15 minutes. He steps back from the table and watches the next shooter hold the dice for an hour, throwing number after number in the hottest roll of the week.

If he could have held his losses down, he would have been in on that roll. Now Bern N. Whole is burning up with anger and looking for a hole to climb into.

Use patience and keep your bets to a minimum until you catch your run. Maybe you won't win the millions you dream of — but a cold streak won't destroy you. And when a streak does appear, you'll be armed with systems that I'll show you later in the book, that will allow you to make a good score.

Listen to me, O ye of little faith and littler bankrolls...

15

WIN GOALS

Stop right here. Don't read these next two chapters until you are wide awake, fresh, and willing to absorb the complete message that is contained on these next few pages. So take a cold drink, clear your mind, and then prepare to accept these words of infinite wisdom.

For you veterans who have read all my previous books, you are aware of what I'm gonna say, but it won't hurt you to pick-up this reinforced reminder.

These two chapters: "Win Goals" and "Loss Limits" are the two most important ones in the whole book — **bar absolutely none!!**

When you gamble — whether at a track, with a bookie, in a Bingo hall, or in a casino — you MUST set your "Win Goal." That is an amount of money you want to win that day. Just walking up to the tables and playing until the bus leaves is flirting with disaster.

Using a watch and saying: "I'll play for an hour and quit — win or lose" is a juvenile statement. Suppose you're in a scorching run and you're winning hand after hand, but your hour is up. Does that mean you must leave that table because your 'time' is up? Of course not. That's a stupid thing to do, yet I see that happen over and over.

Ty M. Toeat has been jumping from table to table, constantly losing, is out $650 and climbs up to a stool at his last table. He starts playing Blackjack and soon catches a scorching roll. For two hours he keeps banging out wins and has recovered practically all his losses. The dealer can do

40

nothing right.

All of a sudden Ty M. Toeat looks at his watch and bellows: "Holy mackeral, it's 7 p.m., I'm late for dinner — I gotta go eat."

He grabs his chips and runs off to fill his empty gut. He oughta plug the hole in his empty head. Never leave a table when you're on a roll — never, never, never, ever, never, ever, never!!!!

I can remember years ago in Vegas when I'd play for 4 days straight at a poker game, because I was on some long hot roll. Every two or three hours I'd just grab some coffee, maybe order a sandwich, walk around the block to clear my head and jump back in. The 'bread' of life will always be there — the 'hot rolls' of gambling are tough to find.

When you enter the casinos you must set this Win Goal and it must be based on your starting Bankroll. It is a percentage return and the amount you will not like, cause it sounds so small to you.

The Win Goal is 20% — like it or not. I personally set Win Goals of 10%, but I am trying to reach the multitude of people who bring down small Bankrolls and must raise the goal to 20% to keep your interest. You'd slam the book shut if I asked you to look for a Win Goal of 10%. At least the 20% figure keeps you with me a few more pages. It *doesn't* mean you will quit when you reach 20%, but that is your goal.

A lot of people head for the casinos with $200 and swear to say the Rosary every day for the next 4 months if they could just win $50. They get ahead $75 and go for the left wing of the casino. Naturally they pour back their wins and then their Bankrolls and spend the ride home thinking of other religions to join — 'cause God let them down.

Without the Win Goal being set, there is no way you

can win consistently. The hard part is sticking to that goal, 'cause sometimes it'll come so quick, but that's the tough part of gambling.

OK, let's take a typical case. Suppose you bring $450 to the casino, set a Win Goal of 20% and follow the rules. That's $90 you are looking to bang them for.

You break that $450 into three separate Sessions of $150 each and go to the first table with $150. Your Win Goal for that Session is 20% ($30). Let's assume you win your $30. Your goal has been accomplished, but you don't wanna leave that table cause you're in a hot trend.

Take the $30 and break it in half. You put the $150 Session money in your pocket, plus half of the $30 Win Goal, which is now called your 'Guarantee.' No matter what happens, you're 'Guaranteed' to show a $15 profit from that Session.

The other half of that $30 is kept in play at that table. It is called your 'Excess.' This 'Excess' allows you to continue competing at this hot table. A new 'Series' starts and when it ends, let's say you show a $28 profit from that Series. Fourteen dollars goes in your pocket with the 'Guarantee' and fourteen dollars stays with your 'Excess' — which is now up to $29.

Another Series bangs out·a $12 profit and again you split it 50-50 with the Guarantee and the Excess getting $6 each. You stay at that table as long as your 'Excess' stays alive. When you start to lose, grab what you can of what's left of the Excess and put it with the 'Guarantee.'

The 'Guarantee' will have at least the original $15 from the Win Goal, plus 50% of every subsequent winning 'Series' after the Win Goal was divided in half, plus the chips you grabbed from the 'Excess' before you lost them all back when you started to lose. If the amount of that

'Guarantee' is around the $90 original Win Goal set for that day — you are finished gambling. There is no need to go to the next two Sessions.

Maybe you're at a plus $78 and still need $12 to make your $90. You could go for another Session or you could take the sure pop $78 profit. Wonder what you'll do!!!

Me??? I'd take the sure shot $78 and run, not walk, to the nearest exit. That's Discipline baby and it takes a lot of guts.

Notice that when you reach the Win Goal at that Session, you don't have to wrap up your play, as it may be hard to find another table that has things going for you.

In a later section on Money Management I will repeat the reference to these Win Goals and have separate chapters on the 'Guarantee' and the 'Excess.' For now I want you to understand the necessity and the power of the Win Goals.

I realize the goals are low, but that's the idea. It's important that you reach your goal with realistic (if not low) figures and get in the habit of winning. The amount you win is absolutely unimportant. The bottom line is bringing home a profit.

Pat Onbac is always patting himself on the back and bellowing to all who will listen about how much he was ahead in the casino. Monday it was $2000, Tuesday $1800, Wednesday $750, Friday $2800 and Sunday over $3000.

You ask him how much he took home and the answer is always the same: "Oh, well, I ended up giving it back, but I had them scared every day. I proved I could beat them..."

No he didn't. He DID NOT prove he could beat them. He proved two things:

1) He could get ahead (which is not an impossible task),
2) He proved he was a jerk by giving back his winnings.

The casinos do not fear jerks like Pat Onbac. They will offer him shows, meals, rooms and even pat him on the back and tell him what a great player he is. Anything to keep him in that casino because they know Onbac is gonna give it back.

In summary:

a) Set your Win Goals at a Session...20%,
b) When it's reached, break it in half,
c) Half in your pocket (Guarantee),
d) Half stays on table (called Excess),
e) Keep playing and split every winning Series between the Guarantee and the Excess,
f) Stay at that table as long as Excess is climbing,
g) When you start to lose, grab balance of Excess and put with Guarantee,
h) Decision time: Should you leave or go the next Session (use guts).

Remember that the goal you set in the beginning of the day, is the goal you want for the whole day. It may take one Session of two or three. Important part is that when it comes, or even when you get close to it, look to run. The understanding of the 'Guarantee' and the 'Excess' is of vital importance, but they'll have their own separate chapters later on.

We'll touch back on this subject in the Money Management section, but I suggest you reread this chapter again and again and again and again and...

The formula for winning is starting right here.

16

LOSS LIMITS

No less important than the previous chapter, so don't go dozing off as you skim through these pages. In fact now that I think about it — this chapter is probably more important — cause it stresses the Minimizing of Losses, a key to staying in the game.

It is imperative that you put a limit on the amount of money you lose on a given day and avoid the feeling of absolutely wipe out. Psychologically you will feel worse if you came home broke, than if you lose a portion of your starting Bankroll.

If you took $300 to the casino and lost 40% — or $120 — you'll feel bad, but at least you have $180 that you stick back in the drawer towards your next trip.

However, if you take $120 to the tables and get cleaned, out the thought of total wipe-out gnaws at you and you feel down right rotten, even though it's the same dollar amount as 40% of $300.

All of these things tend to improve your approach to gambling and by themselves seem unimportant. But lumped together give you a hard core, intelligent attack plan.

Naturally your Loss Limit will apply to both your Bankroll and each individual Session, but will have options and variations, depending on how cold a table you're at.

Each casino game has a different Loss Limit, with Blackjack the lowest because it's the most difficult game.

1) BLACKJACK   Loss Limit 40%
2) ROULETTE   Loss Limit 50%
3) CRAPS   Loss Limit 50%
4) BACCARAT   Loss Limit 50% to 60%

Let's briefly discuss this. The above table means that those figures I've shown are the maximum amount you may lose per day or per Session. You can set your own Loss Limits, but they may not exceed the maximum.

Suppose your game is Craps and you bring $600 to battle. Your Loss Limit that day is $300 but you bring the $600 to feel comfortable. Break it down into three separate 'Sessions' of $200 apiece. Each Session has it's own Loss Limit of $100 (which equals the total of $300 for the whole Bankroll). At the first table you play for two hours and are out $70. The table stays cold as far as the way you're playing. You don't have to stay there until you lose $100, because that is the maximum Loss Limit. You can leave and kill that session as soon as you see it is unprofitable for you.

Ima Greenqueen likes to play Blackjack. She takes $200 to a table and sets her Loss Limit at 30% (or $60). In 15 minutes she's down $40 to a scorching dealer. Ima Greenqueen is a dope if she stays there and tries to play to her maximum Loss Limit. The dealer is hot and the key is to realize that and get outta there.

The Loss Limits are merely figures that you will not exceed. You don't have to play right up to them. Also, the amounts I set per game are maximums. You can set your own limit as long as it's lower.

I put a maximum Loss Limit at Blackjack at 40% for a very good reason. Because it's a rough game. Never lose more than 40% of your session money at a table, but you have the option of setting your own limits.

You could set 35%, 33%, 30%, 25%, 20%, 15%, or 10% — whatever you choose. Bottom line is that you do set that figure and stick to it.

If you lose the first 4 hands at a session — get moving. You're at a cold table and that session is over, regardless of what you set as your Loss Limit.

I know these restrictions are hard on you, but I'm trying to teach you how to get in the habit of winning. Restricting your losses is a big step in accomplishing that.

Look at the front cover of this book and every book I've written. In the upper right hand corner are the words: "Learn How to Win." That's the key, man, 'Learning How to Win.' If you can't follow the strict rules that it takes to win, then you're a dope and always will be. The casinos use the sophisticated approach and calls you a 'gentleman loser.'

I use the 'straight from the shoulder' approach and call you a dope or jerk — same church, different pew.

Kneed X. Citement is an old friend and reads all my books and follows all the rules. He goes to three different Sessions on a particular day. As fate would have it, he catches three hot dealers and drops $120 of the $600 he took to the casino. Now he walks around cursing me out for giving him discipline but taking away his opportunity of getting his thrills at the tables.

This boob doesn't realize that there is no excitement in losing money at gambling tables — only heartache and despair.

You want excitement? Put on a white suit, a white hat, a shiny pair of white boots and drive a white cadillac down the center of Harlem with a big white sign declaring: "Martin Luther King is a Bum."

You'll get all the excitement your lil ole heart can take. You may even come out alive. Now that's excitement!

But when you gamble, approach it as a job, as an exercise of you against the house, cause that's what it is.

Loss Limits will hold down your losses and that's a big, big key to staying in the game.

You can't set Loss Limits and follow them?? Then I can't reach you. And it's only a matter of time before you get whacked.

A final thought. Think over how many times you brought a certain amount of money to a table and did not set a limit on the amount you would lose before quitting. I'll bet most of the time you played down to your last chip, still thinking you're gonna get a streak started and win back all your money. Dreamer...

17

WRAPPING UP BANKROLL

That about bangs up our look at the first part of the Big 4 and naturally it's an important part of our approach.

The things to remember are the key chapters on Win Goals and Loss Limits, but just a last list of reminders to make sure you realize their importance:

a) Bankroll determines every monetary decision,
b) Your starting Bankroll tells you what your Win Goal and Loss Limits are,
c) The idea is to Minimize your losses, waiting for a streak,
d) Look for trends,
e) Break Bankroll into Sessions (preferably 3),
f) Each Session has it's own Win Goal and Loss Limit,
g) Learn How to Win — by accepting small returns,
h) Win Goal — 20%,
i) Break Goal in half once it is reached,
j) Half in your pocket is called your Guarantee,
k) Half on table is called your Excess,
l) Keep playing with that Excess, dividing each subsequent winning series in half,
   (1) This will be covered very, very deeply in Money Management
m) When Excess starts to go — wrap up that Session,
n) Set Loss Limits: In card counting it is 40%,
o) Review the Big 4 and the Little 3,
p) Give this approach a shot — a good one.

Next we move into the 2nd part of the Big 4, but if this part is not absolutely clear, go over it again and again and again and....

KNOWLEDGE OF THE GAME 18

BASIC BLACKJACK

If you're reading a book on card counting, I gotta assume you understand Blackjack. But if you are a novice to this game then the explanation of card counting will go sailing over, through or around your head. I strongly suggest you learn the basic principles, before getting involved with this advanced approach.

I'll keep referring back to my book on Blackjack, which covers the basics and I expect that you have mastered the moves I put in that writing. All of this will come easier to you, if you have a complete grasp of the introduction of my theories.

Black Bart was one of the roughest toughest dudes in the old west, 'cause he was difficult to beat. Same goes for his half brother: Black Jack.

Only I think Black Jack is even rougher because he's almost impossible to beat. Oh sure, you've heard all about how this is the game to play, but I've already explained to you what they meant by that statement.

In the next chapter you'll find a chart that tells you the right moves to make. That is the Basic approach to Blackjack. That is what you *must* know. Ninety percent of the people who play Blackjack do not understand even the basic approach to this game and that's why they get shot down.

To get the tiny intangibles out of the way, let's get real simple for a couple of minutes:

    a) Buy-in means you place cash on the lay out

and the dealers exchange the cash for chips,

b) You can't talk at the table. To indicate whether you will hit or stand: do the following: (I can't believe the number of people who don't know this)

1) To hit: tap the table with your finger,
2) To stand: wave your hand over your cards.

(In Vegas you indicate hit by a sweeping motion with your cards, pulling them towards you. Stand is shown by placing your chips on top of your cards, indicating that you are finished pulling any cards.)

3) Split: Merely place a chip next to your original bet.
4) Double: Exactly the same as split, just lay out a chip.
5) I suggest you keep chatter with dealer to zulch.

Card counting requires strict concentration, so get in the habit of playing strong and silent. In other words, keep your mouth shut. Maybe there are other people at the table that are not particularly interested in listening to your empty chatter with the dealer.

That's the most basic I can get and you should already know this. Just remember what happened to Black Bart when he slipped up. He got a hole in his anatomy. A slip up in Blackjack will get you a hole in your wallet and that smarts too.

19

BASIC STANDING CHART

The chart in this chapter is the complete look at how you should determine your moves of hit, stand, split or double. Many other charts are similar, except that my theory of play is very conservative.

When the dealer is weak, based on his up card, I go for his jugular. When he is powerful, I revert to a conservative style of play, by restricting my double down and split moves. But you'll pick up on this as we go along.

Early on I explained how Julian Braun and John Scarne were probably the men who gave us the most insight into the reasons wht we would hit, as opposed to stand on a certain hand, because of the mathematical edge on the side that gave us the least chance of losing in the long run.

Most of their moves I agree with whole heartedly, but there are some that I deviate from and usually these are moves that offer only a small difference in probable wins or losses — over the long run.

Everyone has to have an awareness of the Basic Strategy approach of this game. It is exactly what it implies: Basic Strategy (basic moves).

For instance, if you have five/two (seven) and the dealer has a king showing as his up card, you don't have to be an A plus student to realize you must hit. In fact one of the facets of the 'Little 3' (Logic) will dictate many of your moves.

I want you to know both the right move and the logical reason as to why you are doing it. After awhile it will

52

HIT ☐ STAND ■ DOUBLE ▨ SPLIT ⊠

YOUR HAND	DEALER'S UP CARD									
	2	3	4	5	6	7	8	9	10	A
8	H	H	H	H	H	H	H	H	H	H
9	H	D	D	D	D	H	H	H	H	H
10	H	D	D	D	D	D	H	H	H	H
11	H	D	D	D	D	D	D	H	H	H
12	H	H	S	S	S	H	H	H	H	H
13	S	S	S	S	S	H	H	H	H	H
14	S	S	S	S	S	H	H	H	H	H
15	S	S	S	S	S	H	H	H	H	H
16	S	S	S	S	S	H	H	H	H	H
A-2	H	H	H	D	D	H	H	H	H	H
A-3	H	H	H	D	D	H	H	H	H	H
A-4	H	H	D	D	D	H	H	H	H	H
A-5	H	H	D	D	D	H	H	H	H	H
A-6	H	D	D	D	D	H	H	H	H	H
A-7	S	D	D	D	D	S	S	H	H	H
A-8	S	S	S	S	S	S	S	S	S	S
A-9	S	S	S	S	S	S	S	S	S	S
A-A	SP	SP	SP	SP	SP	SP	SP	SP	SP	SP
2-2	SP	SP	SP	SP	SP	SP	H	H	H	H
3-3	SP	SP	SP	SP	SP	SP	H	H	H	H
4-4	H	H	H	SP	SP	H	H	H	H	H
5-5	D	D	D	D	D	D	D	D	H	H
6-6	SP	SP	SP	SP	SP	H	H	H	H	H
7-7	SP	SP	SP	SP	SP	SP	H	H	H	H
8-8	SP	SP	SP	SP	SP	SP	SP	SP	SP	SP
9-9	SP	SP	SP	SP	SP	S	SP	SP	S	S
YOUR HAND	2	3	4	5	6	7	8	9	10	A
	DEALER'S UP CARD									

BASIC STRATEGY CHART

53

become second nature.

The next chapter covers some of the differences I have over my initial Basic Strategy chart and they will will be explained in detail, but for now I want you to stop and memorize this chart: until you know it backwards and forwards.

The way I view card counting, and the way any strong player looks at it and makes his moves, is all based on the perfect application of the chart he will use. So work on this one until you're perfect — even if it is a little different.

20

VARIATIONS OF CHART

Before we get to the variations of moves at a Blackjack table, based on the running count, I just want to go over some of the changes I have made on my Basic Strategy chart. The changes are:

a) Ten vs. dealers 2 . . . . Hit
b) Eleven vs dealers 2 . . . . Hit
c) A-A vs dealers 2 . . . . Hit
d) 4-4 dealers 4 . . . . Split
e) 5-5 dealers 2 . . . . Hit
f) 8-8 dealers 10 . . . . Hit
g) 8-8 dealers A . . . . Hit
h) 8-8 dealers 9 . . . . Hit

These are eight moves that I would like to see you change from your previous decisions, to what I have shown above. I ain't gonna tell you that I ran 4 billion hands against the computer, because it'd be a lie.

I can hardly tell a computer from a commuter. All I know is that one is trained to run off decisions and the others runs off decisions on a train.

Where my decisions are reached are down in the pits baby, sitting at the table and trying to minimize my chances of losing. And these eight moves are glaring situations, where I have changed my move to further enhance my play against the house.

a) **TEN VS. DEALERS 2:** Realize that the two, as the

dealers up card, does not mean he is bobbing and weaving. He is weak, but not to the point where he can't recover and bop you. The fact that you get only one card with the double down, leaves you vulnerable to his draw, with the potentially dangerous two.

b) **ELEVEN VS DEALERS 2:** Same as with the 10 vs the two. I don't like laying out extra money, getting only one card and having that dealer pull to a two.

c) **A-A VS THE DEALERS 2:** Combination of reasons as outlined in first two changes. But the extra point here is that you have two gorgeous aces, that contain multiple flexibility moves. It's like having a combo date with Sophia Loren and Raquel Welsh and splitting them, hoping to land Dolly Parton and Miss Universe. Instead, you're dealt Gravel Gertie and Olive Oyl. Stick with Sophia and Raquel and the two aces. You know what you have, and they're both powerful pairs — but's that another story.

This switch of hitting two aces vs the 2 is strongly recommended.

d) **4-4 VS DEALRS 4:** Kind of self-explanatory. By splitting the fours, you now end up with two hands, starting with a four vs the dealer, who is no stronger than you are, with his 4. Plus the fact that you are looking to draw an ace, five, six or seven, which allows you to double down vs his four. Also, you have two separate hands to play for that potential double down opportunity. In Vegas you could also look for a four, which then gives you the chance to split again. I urge you to give this a second look, as it offers you the opportunity to get a lot of money against that dealer when he has his third weakest card (the four). There are times when you'll get two double downs after the split, giving you four times your original bet.

e) **5-5 VS DEALERS 2:** Same explanation as regular 10

vs the four.

f) **8-8 VS DEALERS 10:** This will take a little explaining, so put your thinking caps on. Since I adhere so strongly to the idea of minimizing losses, it is only natural that if I am dealt 8-8 vs the 10, I would either have to hit the 16 and suffer the possibility of losing my $5 approximately 77% of the time with a neutral deck, or ending up with an eight vs a ten...twice. You see, if you split the eights, you now have 8 vs a 10 and 8 vs a 10. You got it twice.

Based on the laws of probability, you will lose 62% of the time that you have an eight vs the dealers ten. So it comes to decision time. Would you rather:

    1) Lose $5 . . . . . . .77% of the time by hitting the 16,

    2) Lose $10 . . . . .62% of the time by splitting.

After the countless hours of participation and looking at the logical side of it, and applying the realization that most people in a casino play with short or scared money, my decision to hit the 16, rather than split, was a rather easy thing to accept. When the shoe has not reached a determination of rich or poor, then I suggest hitting the 8-8 rather than splitting.

I would rather lose $5 seventy seven percent of the time, than lose $10 sixty two percent of the time. And I feel very strongly about this. What's your theory? One way or the other, make your decisions and stick to it.

Maybe this one little example shows you how strongly I feel about minimizing losses.

g) **8-8 VS DEALERS ACE:** Definitely go for the hit, rather than the split, for the reasons stated for the move against the 10. But there is another reason. I am a firm believer in the power of the ace. When I have one of them, I'm happy, and when I have two, the tendency is to start counting my profits.

On the other hand, when the dealer shows an ace, a sinking feeling pops into my gut. And I'm sure you feel the same way. So let's do something about it. Get past the hand and keep your losses down. To do that, simply take your hit and concentrate on the next hand. Splitting the eights gives you $10 at risk, with 8 vs ace and 8 vs ace. Strong feeling towards taking a hit.

h) **8-8 VS DEALERS 9:** Same type of thinking as the two eights vs the dealers ten. I hate splitting those eights and now match up against his nine on two separate hands. Going in, he has the edge on both of my hands, when I split. My chart says to hit those eights and get on to the next hand. Take a minute, put your thinking cap on and see which way you are leaning.

There you have eight moves that I have made towards changing the basic strategy approach that I showed in my Blackjack book. A lot of these changes are from actual playing, and some input was based on my obligation to take into consideration the fact that most people (aside from the professional gambler) do not play enough hands of Blackjack, to allow the laws of probability to set a pattern.

Think you may come around to my thinking on all of these changes.

Before you make your decisions, look deeper into my explanations and try to grasp the reason I give for these swing overs.

You don't have to tell me that every book ever written is in complete disagreement with my theories, I'm well aware of it!

I don't give a rat's tail what other opinions are. I am trying to give you a different look at Blackjack and backing off when the dealer is holding the hammer. It's the way I play, and it is both effective and rewarding.

When you're face to face with your adversary and he has the bigger muscles "'tis better to turn and run away and live to breathe another day."

These examples fit that mold. Take the smallest loss you have open to you and wait for the chance to have the hammer.

21

TWO ACES

While we're kicking around the Theory of basic strategy, let's get right to a move that I almost demand that people do, and hang the fact that each person has their own Theory on this particular play. This is a pet peeve of mine.

It concerns your hand when you are dealt two aces. Since the ace is the most powerful card in the deck, due to it's flexibility, everyone feels a lot better when they're dealt this one-eyed powerhouse.

However, it has been handed down since the days of Adam and Eve that you always split aces. I don't buy that garbage. Here you are sitting with the most powerful card in the deck — in fact two of them — with the chance to make either or both a one or an eleven and you give that edge back to the house.

Hey baby, that's power. You're sitting in the cat-bird seat. If you glance at the dealer's card and he shows a 3 through 7, you know he's in trouble, so the proper move is to make him squirm twice as much. You plop another chip on the lay-out, to indicate you're splitting your hand. Now you have twice as much money against your enemy. That's a good move, whether you win or lose. The percentage of his breaking has the dealer in a weakened position and you took advantage of it by splitting and getting more money against him when he was in trouble.

But, it he shows 9-10-Jack-Queen-King or Ace as his up card, he's the one with the loaded gun.

If you split aces, you're gonna get only one card. Since there are only 13 cards (ace thru King) that you can get as your draw, you're in a position to get dealt an ace, two, three, four, five or six. Where the heck you doing with those dog hands? And you'll get one of those rotten cards six out of thirteen times — by average.

Suppose he has a queen and you split those aces against the queen and catch a five on one hand and a deuce on the other (and the odds are 50-50 you will), where the heck do you thing you're heading?

Probably on the road to two straight losses! With his up card of queen, he is sitting pretty. All he has to do is expose his down card and the odds are he'll whack you.

If he turns over ace, king, queen, jack, ten, nine, eight or seven, you're gonna lose — with both hands. That's 8 out of 13 times he'll shoot you down, just by turning a card over.

He could still turn over a 2, 3, 4, 5 or 6 thus giving him a breaking hand. But one out of those five times he'll draw to either a 17, 18, 19, 20 or 21, and down you go again.

That comes to 9 out of 13 times that he'll whack you.

Lend me your ear!!! I condone splitting aces vs the dealers 3-4-5-6-7 because he is weak. Against the dealers 2 thru 9, and 10-Jack-Queen-King-Ace, I'd like you to hit.

There is an option on the eight. I lean towards the hit, but splitting is not frowned upon. My old chart says split, but my heart says hit.

You decide what part of me you wanna listen to. My heart is black and my head is empty, so whichever way you choose, you have a great excuse to throw rocks at me if things turn out bad.

Seriously, give a lot of thought to this move. I strongly adhere to the fact that two aces should be hit when he has

8 through Ace, or a deuce as his up-card.

One quick side note. I receive many, many, many letters, comments and calls from players who have swung over to this type of thinking and have really improved their game.

Hope you'll do it. You'll see what a strong move this turns out to be.

22

TENS AND ELEVENS

I don't wanna spend a lot of time with this explanation, as the previous chapter made it pretty clear where I stand.

I strongly believe that two aces, elevens and tens should be hit against the dealers power cards of 9 through ace, and not split or doubled down.

Ken I. Count didn't fare too well in arithmetic back in P.S. 22. He took my Blackjack course a couple of years ago and while he wasn't too swift with the numbers, he was a really nice guy and tried to absorb the whole system.

He agreed right off that he didn't want to double the eleven or the ten against the dealers 9 thru ace, but he did want to split the aces against those up-cards.

It took hours and hours of eyeball to eyeball explanation to reach Ken I. Count. In fact I counted 143 separate examples, before the light came on.

He didn't like to double down the eleven vs the dealers queen, for instance. But if you split the aces, you have two hands of Ace — Ace. Since you get only one card per ace when you split aces, in reality you are drawing to an eleven.

It tooks days for Ken I. Count to realize that if he didn't like doubling with the eleven vs that queen and getting only one card, he was compounding his move, by splitting aces vs the queen, cause then he was doing it twice, instead of just once.

I hope you're not in his category. If you don't like to double down with the ten or the eleven, then splitting aces merely gives you two hands of eleven. If it's rotten on one side, it's doubly rotten on the other.

If you agree with not splitting aces, which turns into automatic elevens with a split, then you just can't like doubling with a 6-5 (11), cause it's the same situation.

The same is true with the 6-4 (10) vs the 9 thru ace power cards. There is nothing other than the ace or tens, that can give you a great hand when you double the ten. And the dealer has the same chance as you have to turn over those cards.

I hate a hand of ten vs the power cards of 9 thru ace and never double my bet. I suggest a hit and would like you to follow suit.

A lot of times I 'suggest' you do certain things. In this instance? It is not exactly a suggestion...it's an order!!!

23

AVERAGE WINNING HAND

Studies have been made thru the years in casinos all over the world, based on millions of hands, as to what it really takes to win a hand of Blackjack.

The answer makes a lot of sense. The average winning hand in Blackjack is 18½. That means one simple thing. Unless you have at least a 19, you're in a lot of trouble.

Seventeen is a rotten, stinking hand. When I'm dealt a 10/7 for a total of 17, I feel lousy. I know I'll probably lose and usually do. Eighteen is next to 17 and almost as futile a hand.

In isolated instances you can probably name situations where you ended up with a total of 18 for six straight hands and lost each time. And rightfully so — 18 is a lousy hand.

In fact, you even squirm when you're dealt a nice fat 19 against the dealers jack. You remember the endless times the dealer ended up with a 20 and just nipped you.

That's why it's so important to realize when you're in a good position and when you're in a lousy one. Nineteen and up is a comfort zone. Eighteen and lower is a cruddy zone.

Glance at the Basic Strategy chart for a second. Go down to a soft 18 (ace/seven) vs the dealers 10. It calls for a hit. The reason it says hit the soft 18 is because the ace protects you from going over, and because the 18 vs the dealers 10 is a lousy position to be in.

It takes a lot of intestinal fortitude to hit that soft eighteen and a lot of players won't do it. But if they realized how rotten that soft eighteen was, they sure as heck would call for a hit.

Based on Braun's computations on a neutral deck, it is a 'damned if you do — damned if you don't' situation. If you hit the soft 18 vs the dealers 10, you will lose 57% of the time. If you stand, you lose 59% of the time. Hardly much to choose from.

It's like being in a burning building and having to decide whether to jump from the 4th floor onto the sidewalk, or do a swan dive from the 9th floor onto a lawn. Same is true here. Best move is to hit the soft 18. Sure it hurts, but it's the best percentage move, because it lessens your chances of losing that hand.

Since I ain't no expert on flying, I'll let you make the other decision on what floor to make your exit.

One final point. This is an example I give in my classes on Blackjack and Card Counting and it really wakes up a lot of students.

If you go to the casinos and the dealer had a nine as his up card, all day long, you would be demolished (I didn't even give him a ten or ace).

I've shown examples with four decks, six decks, and eight decks, giving the student 18 and the dealer a nine. Over and over the dealer wins, over the long haul.

Point I'm trying to make is this. When the dealer has a power card, all day long, you're cooked. That's why we get so aggressive when he is in trouble with the weak cards as his up-card.

Average winning hand is 18½. Remember that.

24

POWER CARDS

This was covered pretty thoroughly in the previous chapter, but so as not to leave any empty spaces, let's give it a touch.

Every move you make with the two cards you are dealt is based on the dealers up-card. There are only 13 up-cards that could appear: Ace, deuce, three, four, five, six, seven, eight, nine, ten, Jack, Queen, King. Now we'll break it down into a form of a ladder of Blackjack.

a) **9-10-J-Q-K-Ace:** dealer is strong and will probably whack you,

b) **7-8:** He isn't strong. He isn't weak. We'll call him neutral,

c) **2-3:** Again: He isn't that weak, but naturally he isn't sitting with a gun to your head. Give him a little respect and call it a stand-off, or even neutral,

d) **4-5-6:** He's in trouble and you have to double and split against these weak cards as much as you can.

It doesn't take a mathematical genius to realize that eliminating four Neutral cards, where the dealer is neither weak or strong, leaves three situations where he's in trouble and six situations where you are. That's not an even fight. It puts you in trouble twice as much as him.

67

That's why I want as many double down and split moves as possible against the 4-5-6. Because six times out of thirteen he is powerful and that is one of the reasons I want you to fear this game.

Think of it: out of the 13 cards the dealer could give himself as his up-card, six times he has you against the wall.

And unless you're paint or wall paper, that's a lousy place to be.

25

SOFT HANDS

I've given lectures at places where a guy will stand up, admit he's been playing Blackjack for 15 years and stare blankly into space when I ask him what he'd do with a soft 16 against the dealers seven.

Invariably he'll ask: "What's soft mean?" The temptation is to tell him: "That part of your brain that allows you to play Blackjack without knowing what a soft hand is."

Recently I was speaking at a men's club in South Jersey and a self proclaimed Blackjack wizard made a remark very loudly — so that everybody within 8 miles could hear: 'that he never has lost in Blackjack and he's been going to the casinos for seven years.'

Right away I knew I had my pigeon. I asked him to stand up and give me his name. Cockily, he announced his name was Idun Know and just as cockily he repeated the statement that he never lost at Blackjack.

I asked him 3 questions concerning the game and Idun Know didn't know what I was talking about. His answers were all the same:

a) What is a soft hand? . . . . "I dunno."
b) Against what cards do you double
    with a soft 14? . . . . "I dunno."
c) Can you have a 4 card soft hand? . . . "I dunno."

He was a jerk and before the night was over, everybody within ear shot knew it. The answers in order are:

a) Any hand that has an ace where the next card can't break you,
b) vs the dealers 4-5-6,
c) yes: ace, two, three, four, is a soft 20 or a hard 10 (use it as a 20).

But he isn't an isolated case. A lot of people don't realize what the term soft means.

Anytime you have an ace in your hand the total is soft, until you reach the point where a card could break you. Some examples:

1) Ace/deuce . . . . .soft 13
2) Ace/nine . . . . .soft 20
3) Ace/seven . . . . .soft 18
4) Ace/four/four . . . . .soft 19
5) Ace/four/seven/four . . . . .hard 16
6) Ace/three/eight . . . . .hard 12
7) Ace/ace/two/five . . . . soft 19 or hard 9
8) Ace/four/two/six . . . . .hard 13

Soft hands provide you opportunities to double down. But learn the difference as to when your hand is 'hard' or 'soft.'

Do you know how many times I get asked the question "Can I double a three or four card soft hand?" Of course you can't.

And for you novice novices who wonder how this could come about, without the soft hand occurring in the first two cards, read on. A player could be dealt a two/three vs the dealers five and call for a card. He draws an ace, giving him a soft 16. All he can do is make it a hard six and hit.

Good grief, if you didn't know that, you're in the wrong game.

26

WHY DO YOU DOUBLE?

You think this is a question asked only by novices? Think again. I've heard veteran players rattle profanities as yet undiscovered, when they draw a rotten card on a double down move.

What do they expect — a good card? Odds are they won't get one. That's because the odds are against you getting a good card most of the time.

Stick this statement in a part of your brain that will keep it fresh for use at the Blackjack tables:

"You do not double to get a good card!!! You double to get more money vs the dealer when he's in trouble!!!"

Read that statement over and over and over and let it's meaning sink in. A lot of players think they're supposed to get a great card cause they've doubled their bet. The answer is Nay!

Skip back a few pages to the chapter on 'Average Winning Hands.' The answer was that 18½ was an average winning hand.

Okay, let's say you are a firm believer in the Basic Strategy that is preached by every guy who ever wrote a book on Blackjack. They all state the best move with an Ace/two vs the dealers six is to double down. We'll say that you've just nodded your head in agreement, because that is the proper move.

Let's see what 'could' happen. There are only 13 cards (ace thru King) that the dealer could give you as your 'down' card. With 18½ or higher as your goal, you're looking for:

a) **Eight, seven or six:** Now you have 21, 20 or 19,

b) **Five:** Now you have 18 (Neutral hand),

c) **Four, three or two:** Now you have either soft 17, soft 16, or soft 15, all lousy hands,

d) **Ace:** You have soft 14, again a rotten hand,

e) **King, Queen, Jack or 10:** Worse yet, you have hard 13 on any of those draws,

f) **Nine:** Another stiff hand, hard 12.

See what happens? Out of the 13 cards you could get, only three would give you at least an average winning hand (8-7-6).

The rest of the time you have less than an average winning hand.

That's only 3 out of 13 times you can expect to get a windfall. The rest of the time you're sitting with garbage.

Yet the proper move is to double. All strong Blackjack players do it, even though the odds are 3 to 10 against getting a good hand.

That's because you do NOT double to get a good hand. You double to get more money against the dealer when he's in trouble. Or didn't I say that already?

Remember when I showed you the ladder of Blackjack? Six times the dealer was strong (9 thru Ace) and three times he was weak (4-5-6). That's six to three against you and that ain't healthy odds.

So to make up for that, you wanna be in positions where you can double your bet against him, because he has to hit. And when the dealer hits, it is the only chance he has of breaking.

The way we do that is by doubling down when he's in trouble. So stop worrying about the fact that you'll get a lousy card — cause you probably will.

But now you have twice as much money against your enemy and he *has* to hit. Knowing when to double down is an art and a move that should be taken. I just want you to know why you're doing it.

Hey man, I'd love to double an Ace/two all day long vs the dealers five. And I'd be overjoyed if I was given just a deuce as my draw card. That would only give me a hand of hard five or soft fifteen to fight that dealer. But he *has* to hit and therein lies my edge.

Know what to do, when to do it, and why you're doing it...

Based on the intelligence level of the players in most casinos, you'll stand out as a great player if you know those three things.

27

SPLITTING

The Theory behind the reason you split two cards of equal value is the same type of reasoning that applies to Doubling: To get more money bet against the dealer when he's in trouble.

At the risk of repeating myself, which I will do many, many, many times in this book, it's important you get the drift.

The dealer is powerful with the 9 thru Ace as his up-card and we do not split against those cards. Exceptions are as follows:

a) You may split two eights vs dealers 9, if that is how you wish to handle this move, but I have already suggested you hit that 16, even though it is a rotten position to be in,

b) Split two nines vs the dealers nine. That puts you right even with that dealer with your two hands vs his one.

That's it! That's the only time you split vs power cards, and I hit my 8/8 against the nine.

Another plus is the fact that you can double after a split. If you're dealt two sixes vs the dealers six, you're sitting in the catbirds seat. When you split your sixes, you have a chance of getting an Ace, two, three, four, or five and can now double down.

Suppose a five dollar bet is made. You're dealt two sixes, which you split. You catch an Ace on the first one.

74

Double down. Then the second six catches a deuce. Again double down.

That $5 wager ballooned into a $20 bet against the dealers weak six and that's the position you want him in, all day long.

Then we come to two picture cards and the obvious question: "Can I split tens?" Hey baby, you can jump off the Brooklyn Bridge and I can't stop you. But ask me SHOULD I jump...? or SHOULD I split tens and the answer is NO!!!

Claire A. Taable loves to play Blackjack, but hasn't the foggiest idea of the difference between a good move and a bad one. One thing she has pounded into her pea brain is that whenever you're dealt two similar cards, you split.

Even when she is dealt two tens, she slides up that extra chip to indicate split. With those two tens she was dealt, she has a 90% chance of winning.

You'll hear the stupid cries of the novice, who falls back on the fact that the dealer is in trouble and you must split. The other side of the coin comes into play. You'd split sevens against the dealers six because two sevens constitute a rotten hand. Splitting is a smart move.

But the two tens are not a rotten hand. They're a powerful force to have going for you and chances are you'll win that hand.

Yeah, you'll antagonize every decent player at that game where two tens are split and they'll probably leave that game.

If you wanna clear a table of players, do what Claire A. Taable does and split them. A stupid move.

In Atlantic City there are more opportunities to split and double down than in most other casinos throughout the world. Learn when and how to take advantage of these moves.

As we get deeper into card counting, you'll see the variations of moves you will make in splitting situations, to take advantage of the richness or poorness of a deck or shoe.

28

CHARTING A TABLE

Now we elaborate on the previous chapter and re-emphasize the importance of this move.

Gambling is an exercise — performed by millions of people — in an attempt to win money. And don't hand me that garbage that it is done for entertainment.

Once we accept the reason for our NEED for gambling, an intelligent 'Logical' approach should be followed. Whatever 'Theory' you might have (aggressive or conservative) the bottom line is looking for a 'Trend' to develop.

Notice how the "Little 3" has a bearing on how you approach the game? Now, let's see how the Big 4 comes into play.

In order to compete, you must have the "Bankroll" to stay in the game until that 'Trend' comes. When it comes you sure as heck better know everything there is to know about that particular game. That's "Knowledge of the Game."

Strict "Money Management" methods will show you how to 'Minimize' your losses and then when that hot streak pops up — your "Money Management" will show you how to bet — in order to get the most out of a good run.

Since you set a 'Win Goal' and a 'Loss Limit' when you sat at a particular 'Session,' the 'Discipline' of knowing when to quit has already been predetermined and will lock up 'Guaranteed' wins at good tables.

The 'Excess' approach or 'Theory' allows you to go for bigger returns.

Notice how everything I elaborated upon before must tie together and feed off of each other in order to give us just a 50-50 chance of winning.

In Blackjack we must have something to help us key on the streaks a certain dealer may be in. The way we do that is by charting his streaks. Since the 9 through ace as his up card puts him in a power position, I don't want you sitting at tables when they are constantly his show card.

It prohibits doubling and splitting opportunities and the only way to avoid fighting those cards is to stay away from tables where he is in a streak of showing them.

Now this is for both the basic player and the card counter, with one exception. It is the ONLY factor the basic player has to go on, so he shouldn't ever play at a table without this simple charting method.

On the other hand, the card counter will use this method, plus something you will learn later called Back Counting. Don't worry about it just yet. Just remember that the counter has two ways to look for a streak, the basic player has only one way.

Here's how to chart a table:

1) You've decided to play Blackjack,
2) Find a section of tables that fit your Bankroll,
3) Chart tables only where there is at least two empty seats, so that you can sit down if shoe is in your favor,
    (a) Bye N. Tyme is a great charter of tables. He spends an hour charting a table and counting the deck and finds a rich count of 86. He goes to sit down and take advantage and finds there are no empty

seats. The dope wasted all that time charting a table that did not offer the chance
to play. Don't waste time at a full table.

4) Card Counters may chart tables only where
first base is open. We'll go into this later,
regarding sitting at first base.

5) Concentrate only on what the dealer's single
up card is (not the eventual outcome of the
hand),

6) All decisions are made vs that up-card, so you
wanna play only at a table where you have a
dealer showing weak up-cards.

Here's how to determine his strengths and weaknesses:

(a) 9 through ace . . . . He's strong.
(b) 7-8 . . . . . Neutral: Not strong, but not weak.
(c) 2-3 Neutral: Weak, but in a position to draw.
(d) 4-5-6 . . . . Weak

7) Look for imbalance of weak cards to strong,
based on 10 hands.

8) If more strong cards to weak cards, leave and
begin charting another table.

9) If first 3 cards are strong....walk away.

NOTE: For you hecklers reading this page right now,
you could say that if you charted a table and sat down, it
would change the flow of the cards and possibly lure you
to a table where the dealer would start getting strong cards.
My comment to you is: 'hog-wash.' We're looking for patterns that a dealer may be in and every little thing we do to
catch an edge is in our favor. If you won't chart a table —
don't play Blackjack, period.

Here are some examples from which to draw: (shows
series of dealer's up card and what you should do.)

	UP-CARD	**DECISION**
1)	Ace, nine, queen	move on
2)	Ace, three, five, seven	play
3)	four, five, ten, jack, eight, two, nine, six, three	play
4)	nine, ten, four, four, seven, eight, ten, three, jack	move on
5)	five, seven, queen, eight, six	play
6)	nine, seven, four, eight, jack, ace, five, king	move on
7)	king, queen, five, ten, eight, three, six, eight, four, ten	move on
8)	king, queen, eight, seven, king, jack	move on
9)	five, nine, three, two, ten, six	play
10)	three, ten, five, queen, seven, nine, four, jack, eight, ten	move on

Notice I lean more to moving on than I do to playing. Fact is, I'm looking not to play until I find a dealer running cold. It doesn't bother me to chart 12-15 tables until I find a cold dealer with an opening at first base.

After you find the table to play at, keep an eye on the dealers up-card and watch the pattern. By now you're governed by your pre-determined Win-Goals and Loss Limits, and they will determine how long you compete at that Session.

Charting a table is a big, big factor in playing Blackjack. I waited until the end to tell you of the importance of this chapter. Mark your book that this is a chapter that should be re-read often. It shows the tie-in with all the things I stress.

I'll refer back to this chapter a couple more times, so bend the page in order to make it easy to find. Charting a table is a MUST.

29

ETCH E. PANTS

Ever see Etch E. Pants on his way to the casinos? I'll concentrate on Atlantic City for now cause he usually cuts me off on the Parkway as I head there myself.

He moves in and out of traffic, chomping at the bit to get to the tables. Any car in his way is cut off and he shouts obscene things to the driver of the other car for delaying his playing time.

Three times a month he gets caught in the speed trap in South Jersey, but that doesn't deter him. He blames the troopers for their part in the conspiracy to delay his gambling.

When he goes by bus, he stands the last 60 miles cause he wants to be the first one off the bus.

On the days when traffic is heavy and it takes a few extra minutes to reach A.C., he hops out the window and runs the last 17 miles — afraid that the tables will be closed if he's a little late.

Breathlessly, he races into a casino, money burning a hole in his pocket. He sees an empty seat at a Blackjack table and makes a bee-line for the spot.

He doesn't bother to chart the table to see if the dealer is hot or cold. Little does he know that she is engulfed in a hot run, having won 14 straight hands including 6 straight Blackjacks.

Etch E. whips out his total Bankroll of $275 and buys in. His socks roll down to his shoes as the dealer gives him eleven $25 chips.

Etch E. didn't realize he was at a $25 table. But he's too embarassed to leave, so he acts like the $25 bet is something he makes every day.

The dealer stays hot and despite getting four straight 19's Etch E. loses the first four hands.

Figuring he can't lose forever, he doubles his bet to $50. Voila!!! He gets two sevens vs the dealers 6. Happily, he slides another $50 on the table to signify a split. He gets a three for a total of 10. Now he hesitates.

The cute little dealer smilingly says: "You have 10 sir, do you wish to double down?" Etch E. is now itching all over his seat. Sweat pouring down his back, he slides out another $50 for the double down. He gets a king for a total of 20 and breathes a little easier.

Moving to the other 7, the dealer again bangs out a 3 and again looks to Etch E. for a double down bet. He can't even swallow, let alone move.

He has only one $25 chip left out of his buy-in of $275, but the other people at the table are looking at him and he can't let his ego down, by playing scared.

He reaches into his pocket and pulls out two tens and three singles and is still $2 short. Etch E. goes to his pocket and pulls out a handful of change, counts out $1.75 which he embarrassingly pushes in front of him.

He asks the dealer if she'll accept an IOU or the two stamps he'd like to put up. She shakes her head no. The irritated patron in the next seat slams a quarter on the table: "Let's play."

Now everybody at the table knows Etch E. Pants is on the brink of disaster. But the fickle finger of fate points good fortune in the direction of our hero. The dealer hits Etch E. with another king, giving him two hands of 20, and $200 in bets against the dealers weak 6.

Etch E. is already counting his winnings as the dealer turns over her hidden card and shows a four, giving her a total of 10. Etch E. sweats a little more, squirms a little more, prays a little more and dies a little more.

He has good reason, as that fickle finger of fate pokes him in the eye. The dealer turns over the ace of hearts and breaks Etch E. Pants' heart. She has a total of 21.

Etch E. is stunned as he slides off the stool — broke. He has played five hands in five minutes and in that time broke every rule possible as to approaching a game. Even though every one of his hands was either 19 or 20, he did everything wrong as to checking out that table.

As he heads for the door, his companions from the bus are just arriving. "Hey, Etch E., you sure run fast. Bet you're just itching to get started..."

The ball of cotton in his mouth prevents him from answering. His mind is exploring things to do to kill 6 hours until the bus leaves.

He decides to run home, hoping to get a heart attack and put him out of his misery. But he figures his luck is so bad that he'd get a ticket for going thru the tolls without money and end up in jail instead of dying.

Do you know any Etch E. Pants, or are you one?

This is a true story — only the name of the bridge he eventually jumped off is deleted. And it happens every day, in every casino. Only the amounts of money and the names of the people change.

Heed the message...O Ye Of Little Discipline.

30

WHAT IS CARD COUNTING?

If you're reading a book on card counting, it's fairly obvious you want to become a proficient Blackjack player.

I just want to be on record as telling you what a rough game it is, as opposed to Roulette, Craps or Baccarat.

And if you're going to play this game, you've already heard that the card counter has reduced the 1.52 edge against the strong basic strategy player, to a neat 2% in favor of the counter.

But, you gotta be a perfect counter. So get yourself prepared for heavy concentration, although the actual part of counting is a snap.

Here's the reasoning behind card counting. It is the Theory of professional Blackjack players that when there are more picture cards in the deck, as opposed to small cards, then the deck is rich in 10's, and thereby beneficial to the player.

That's because the player must make his hitting or standing decisions before the dealer and knowing when your chances of getting a picture card is increased, because the deck is rich, helps you to make stronger decisions. It also helps to know when the deck is poor or short in ten valued cards. You can adjust your basic strategy to coincide with this imbalance.

Suppose we're playing Blackjack on the train coming home from work with a group of guys and a single deck is being used. Everyone has a good knowledge of the game.

Pritt E. Solit is a pretty solid player with a strong ap-

proach to the right moves. Sitting next to him is Hyma
Kounter, who is a polished card counter.

They are both dealt fourteen vs the dealers up card of
nine. Pritt E. Solid, knowing basic strategy, hits his 14.
Hyma Kounter, already aware that of the remaining half
deck of cards to be dealt, there are 13 tens sitting in that
group, opts for a stand.

The other players think he's a jerk 'cause every good
player knows you must hit all breaking hands against the
standing cards of seven thru ace. They smugly smile to
themselves at Hyma's ignorance.

It ain't ignorance. He knows that there were 16 ten
valued cards when the deck began and only three came
out so far. That left 13 still sitting in the dealers deck.

The chances of drawing a ten and busting that hand of
14 has increased, so the card counter will adjust his basic
strategy and stand, rather than buck the odds against him.

Pritt E. Solit has a pretty good possibility of drawing a
ten and getting whacked. I know, I know, I know!!! If the
desk is rich, there's a good chance the dealer has a ten hidden and will beat you by just turning his hidden card over.

True, but let's look at the logic:

 a) If you positively knew that your chances of
    drawing a ten card had increased, you're not
    gonna go looking for trouble by drawing,
 b) That hand of 14 is rotten to begin with, even
    with a neutral deck. Now that you are sure of
    an imbalance against you, another point is the
    fact that even a 9 or 8 could also break you,
 c) By holding back and not taking the hit, there
    is the possibility that the dealer could turn
    over his down card and show a 2, 3, 4, 5 or
    6, putting him in the same position as you (a

breaking hand). But now he *must* hit and since the deck is rich, he'll probably catch a ten.

You see the thinking in utilizing even the tiniest of edges towards decreasing your chances of losing? All these little things add up. I personally use card counting to add a new wrinkle to my basic strategy.

I believe that card counting is getting to use all the little things we can find, in order to allow us to make stronger hitting or standing decisions.

The next chapter tells you how to use card counting in conjunction with the way you think.

31

HOW TO USE CARD COUNTING

Here's where I differ from the main stream of people who teach card counting. Maybe some of you have heard how these other people use card counting to tell them when the deck is rich and use that Knowledge to increase their bets.

What they are preaching, is that when the deck becomes rich in tens, the imbalance is in favor of the player and they should now start increasing the amounts of their wagers.

As the count goes higher, the deck or shoe is now becoming richer. The bets become bigger and bigger, based on this climbing count.

That is their 'Theory' on how to play and since 'Theory' is opinion, who am I to argue with their Knowledge? After all, they are card counters, have perfected the game and believe this is the way to use that Knowledge.

They feel you should bet $5 hand after hand and then when the deck reaches the count that indicates the deck is rich in picture cards, they suggest increasing your bet to $25, or $50, or $75.

I don't buy that. It's just that I feel that minimizing losses, having a proper Bankroll and managing your money on a stricter scale is a better approach. Suppose you're sitting at a table and the count has not as yet reached the 'rich point.' You are told to bet $5 a hand — the minimum.

Then the count indicates a rich situation has taken hold

and the shoe has a strong compliment of tens, as opposed to smaller cards.

Unfortunately, you've lost 7 of the past 10 hands and are in a kinda bad trend. How can you tell somebody who has just lost that many hands, to up his next bet to $50? I don't buy it.

I use card counting to improve my Basic Strategy, both from knowing when the deck is rich in tens and poor in tens. I'll get into variations of the betting patterns in the Money Management section. But I want you to know where I'm coming from, as to the use of card counting.

32

MY SYSTEM

There are various ways to count cards and different systems are invented each year, each containing the theory of the author of that particular method.

Some use a plus - minus system, some are based on a running count, some are actual counts, some eliminate the 6, 7 and 8, some just one of those numbers. Some systems count the ace as 10, others as plus one, and some others as 0.

Many systems use a combination of true count to running count, based on the number of approximate decks left in the shoe, which is arrived at by taking a guess as to how many cards are in the discard tray and subtracting that amount from the total number of decks used, taking into consideration how many cards are behind the cut card.

Enough already — or did all that make sense to you? It didn't do a thing for me.

Once I came across a system that was as easy as mine. It was invented by a foreign nobleman named Count Hire N. Loher III.

It involved counting only the red cards that were dealt, and dividing that total by the seat you were sitting in and adding your age, plus ½ the amount of the bet by the player at third base, if he was over 50. If there is a woman at third base, leave the table, the system won't work.

I thought the method was fabulous until I read the fine print at the bottom of the page. It only worked on Tuesday and Thursday in casinos in Puerto Rico.

You'll have no problem finding systems claiming to make you rich. Mine won't. What it is designed to do is:

a) Reduce your chances of losing,
b) Improve your Basic Strategy,
c) Keep you abreast of the imbalance between ten value cards and non-tens,
d) Get you to utilize a shoe rich in tens,
e) Get you to utilize a shoe poor in tens,
f) Show you a side count of aces,
g) Give you a couple edges in a rough game,
h) Reduce your chances of losing, or did I already say that.

And please, please don't tell me that the use of six or eight decks and the burying of two decks, white washes all the plusses of card counting.

No, it doesn't. Regardless of the amount of decks, you'll still catch imbalances between tens and non-tens.

The two decks frozen behind the cut card are 'averaged' and taken as two full neutral decks. Since you'll never see what they were, you treat them as if they do not exist and figure that over periods of time they will in fact turn out to be of average effect, one time hurting you and the next time helping.

The house does it to cause effect, so there's no use worrying about it. When you play against a single deck, where they deal to the last card, you have a license to steal. So it's only natural that some type of steps must be taken to slow down the counter.

Before we get too deep, let's take this thing in stages. Let's get to what this chapter is all about: My System, and here it is.

   a) All tens, jacks, queens and kings get a minus 2,

   b) Ace, deuce, three, four, five, six, seven, eight and nine get a plus one,

   c) We'll keep a side count of aces.

That's it!!! That's the whole system of counting. Oh, I'll get into reasons, speed drills and variations of moves, but the system itself is as simple as A, B, C (above).

Okay, after absorbing that whole method of counting, you deserve a break. Take a break.

33

NEUTRAL DECK

When you pick up a deck of cards and lay it out on a table there will always be 52 cards. Sixteen will be ten value cards (10, Jack, Queen, King), and thirty six will be non-tens (Ace, 2, 3, 4, 5, 6, 7, 8, 9).

That means the ratio of small cards to ten value cards is 36-16, or 2¼ to one. This is called a neutral deck.

As the cards are dealt, more small ones may come out. This sets up an imbalance of less small cards to large remaining in the shoe.

Suppose you pick up a neutral deck (36-16) and start dropping cards on the table. Laying out 12 cards you find 15 small ones and 2 tens were dealt.

That leaves 21 small cards and 14 large ones. The ratio of small cards to large now reads 21-14, or 3-2. There are no longer 2¼ small cards to large. For every one of those 15 small ones that came out, there should have been approximately 7 large cards, keeping with the ratio. The fact that these large cards are still in the deck creates an imbalance we call 'rich.'

The deck is now considered 'rich' in picture cards, having moved way off the 2¼-1 ratio, all the way down to 1½-1. That's a big change.

I've already told you that the theory of all card counters is that a shoe, or deck, favoring an overage of 10 valued cards is called 'rich.'

One that has more small cards than large ones, over and above the 2¼-1 ratio is considered a 'poor' deck, simply because it is lower in remaining tens.

Take that same neutral deck and lay eight tens on the table and then pull out 4 small cards. The total number of small cards to large ones now reads 32, matched against 8 tens.

The ratio is 32-8, or 4-1. That's way over the 2¼-1 neutral start. These remaining cards show an imbalance of 4 1, favoring the non-tens, and since this situation is considered not to be in favor of the player, the designation of 'poor' is given to that deck. It is 'poor' in picture cards and/or tens.

Now some of you may say that calling a nine a small card, just like a deuce, is too big a gap since there are six other cards in between. You could claim that since the nine is right next to the ten, the value should be similar.

Please remember that the break must come somewhere and this is the best way to apply the theory and still reach the majority of people who play Blackjack. Your question is well taken, but you'll see the light as we move along.

Remember several chapters back where I said different gamblers had different theories on how to count? Well, I know some tremendously strong counters, that give a value to every single card and can fly thru a deck in 11 seconds.

These are effective systems and give the player a strong edge. But those guys count cards every day and practice hours and hours per week. The majority of people reading this page, don't or won't practice that much. Nor can you do it, due to your job and other commitments. The time needed to apply practice sessions would be wasted, cause you'll probably only get to use it once a month. You'll become rusty.

So the system I preach and teach will not give you a

true, no holds barred, absolute, bonafide, positive, accurate, up to the instant count.

But it will give you a strong indication of the imbalance of small cards to large cards. I use it daily in the casinos, find it tremendously effective and easy to apply and maintain.

In this system, nine is considered low and 10 is considered high. The method is not infallible, but it is very strong. In fact, as you start to perfect and use it, and as the count goes up into the sixties and seventies, or way down in the 1-2-3-4 range, you'll find the count is very, very powerful and opens up a lot of moves.

So bear with me and stop looking for holes in the approach. Remember about the neutral deck — 36-16 ratio of small cards to large. That's 2¼-1. Now let's see how we handle Basic Strategy as the count starts to move.

34

VARIATIONS OF NEUTRAL

OK, you've picked up a deck of cards and as far as counting is concerned, the designation of that deck is called neutral (36-16).

With that ratio at 2¼-1, we are looking for a swing in either direction. If a lot of small cards come out, the count will climb and the deck will receive a code of 'rich,' meaning a lot of ten value cards are left. Large cards coming out gives the remainder of the deck the code of 'poor.'

A few chapters back I told you how simple it was to use this system. All small cards are a plus 1 and all tens are a minus 2.

If you're sitting at a table and three small cards come out, that doesn't mean a big imbalance has set in and you mortgage your house on the next hand. The designation 'neutral deck' stays around for a long time, even though a lot of small cards are dealt.

When you get to the application of counting at a six deck game, you will note that the count will start at 25 and maintain a designation of 'neutral' — all the way through the count of 48. That's a lot of hands, baby.

Based on the plus 1 for every small card and starting at 25, you could have 15 small cards come out, the count could rise to 40 and still be considered 'neutral.' That's the reason the casinos go to the multiple deck method.

In this case it would be classified 'high neutral.' So don't go thinking way ahead of me and don't go trying to absorb the last three paragraphs, as I'll explain this in simpler form later on.

I'll bring you along my way. What is important is that you realize that the term neutral does not just stay with the deck until the number moves off the starting count.

In fact, 80% of the time you'll be playing with a deck called 'low neutral,' 'neutral' or 'high neutral' and with six decks, that count can range anywhere from 20 through 48. That's a lot of territory.

What we're waiting for is that count to move into a strong 'rich' or 'poor' designation and then we make our moves.

35

"RICH AT 49"

Keep the number 49 fresh in your mind. That's the number which keys the fact that the deck has become 'rich' and moves can now be made.

I told you that the theory of card counting was based on the fact that when the deck was rich in tens, the deck or shoe was in favor of the player. But don't get the idea that you're now supposed to win the next five hands just because the shoe is rich.

You are looking to reach that point and my theory is to use it to improve your basic strategy, but get an understanding of how this can help you.

Grab yourself a normal deck of cards. You'll start your count at 45 and turn each card over — one at a time, face up — giving a plus one to every non-ten and a minus two to every ten value card.

Go through the whole deck and you'll end up exactly at 49 every time. In fact, no matter what number you set as your starting count, you'll always end up four notches higher.

I pick 45 as your starting count, so as not to reach the count of zero, whereby you may get into a pattern of minus 1 or plus 3 or minus 6 or plus 2. Your head will be swimming just trying to remember which side of the zero you're on.

Naturally this could never happen with a single deck count, cause even if all 16 large cards came right out, the count could not drop under 13 with the applying of minus two to every ten card.

But when you are playing against a six or eight deck shoe, there will be times that you'll approach zero, cause your six deck shoes will start at a count of 25. For now just remember that the single deck starting count is 45 and the rich mark is 49.

The reason is very simple. Since there are 36 small cards vs 16 large ones, the ratio is 2½-1, based on simple arithmetic. Take the 16 ten value cards out of the deck and lay them on a table. Then take two small cards and place them on top of each ten.

You will have used up 16 tens and 32 non-tens and still have four non-tens left over. By applying the plus one factor to every small card and minus two to every large one, it's only logical that you'll end your count at 49.

The two small cards on top of each ten ends up in a neutral offset, and the four small cards left in your hand raise the count from 45 to 49. Got it???

No matter what number you start with, it'll always end up 4 clicks higher — due to those 4 extra small cards in every deck. That gives us the difference between the ratio of small cards being 2-1 as opposed to 2¼-1.

Since you've already keyed in on the fact that 49 is your 'rich' point, it's very easy to see that the 'rich' designation can come very fast when playing with one deck.

Stretching out the decks to six, you now have four extra cards per deck (24 in all) to be used up before reaching that classification of 'rich.' So the casinos use six decks to make it harder to reach 49, because you must use up so many cards.

We'll get to that later on, but keep it in the back of your mind what we're trying to accomplish with counting and how to use this count.

Many times you'll reach 49 after dealing out only a handful of cards (single deck), which explains why it is so easy to count against one deck and why it is so easy to get to 49 and higher so swiftly.

Grab a deck and start dealing the cards one at a time — all the while stating your count out loud. Suppose these cards are dealt:

3, 5, K, Q, 7, 8, 4, 2, A, 5, 6

Starting with the count of 45, continue to increase or decrease the count as the cards appear:

(45) 46, 47, 45, 43, 44, 45, 46, 47, 48, 49, 50

Eleven cards were dealt and we climbed to 50. Two large cards came out, which means 4½ small cards should have been dealt, according to the laws of probability.

Nine small cards came out and by applying a plus one to each we jumped to 54, minus 2 for both the king and queen, and we're at 50.

In all actuality, we're in a 'rich' position. But since a single deck will very often arrive at 49 so fast, I call it a medium rich and do not drastically change my Basic Strategy. If it happened a little deeper into that deck, that's a different story and I'd have a true rich count. My strategy would be substantially changed.

Same is true if this happened with six decks. A count of 50 signals the player that he is in rich country and adjustments should be made.

OK, drop back a little. You now know what I mean when I say that a deck has reached a rich point (49 or higher). Summing up:

a) Deal out a single deck, one card at a time, face up,

b) When you finish the whole deck, count will be at 49,

c) Repeat the drill, laying cards out one at a time. When count reaches 49 anywhere along the way, you'll know an imbalance has occurred.

Practice with one deck, turning the cards over face-up and applying the plus one minus two count. See how fast you can go and still end up at 49. Gotta start swinging into the speed factor.

36

"POOR AT 35"

Staying with the single deck and the starting count of 45, let's go to the other side of the spectrum. You also want to see when the deck pops into a position of 'poor.'

Since there are two small cards for every large one, it is easy to climb from 45 to 49, because the odds favor the small card (plus 1) appearing 2¼ times more than a ten.

So to reach the point of 'poor,' the same theory would apply. With a single deck, use 35 to come to a classification of 'poor.'

Suppose a hand was dealt and the following cards came out:

A, 8, Q, 10, Q, 3, 10, J, 4, K, 10

Starting at 45, your count would go:

(45) 46, 47, 45, 43, 41, 42, 40, 38, 39, 37, 35

You're at 35 and it was reached thusly: Seven ten value cards came out, dropping the count to 31. Four small ones brought the count to 35. These seven 10 value cards should have produced 15.75 small cards. They didn't, as only four non-tens appeared.

That meant the count dropped to 35 and means there are less ten value cards to pull from, then the original 2¼-1 ratio. The remaining deck now contains 32 small cards and 9 large ones, decidedly over the 2¼-1 ratio.

Your chances of getting a large card is reduced, your chances of getting a Blackjack is reduced, due to the loss of so many 10 value cards, and you can now look for a bevy of non-tens to make the scene.

Just for a moment shoot back to what I said about using the designation 'poor' to help your Basic Strategy.

Playing with a single deck and lodged at a count of 35, I fully expect small cards to appear. My theory is not to just use the count to affect my bet, but to improve by Basic Strategy moves.

Everyone knows you should stand with a 12 vs the dealers 4 thru 6. But, but, but — the counter knows the deck is 'poor' in ten value cards with the count at 35 and the chances of catching a breaking ten has now been reduced. I will hit my 12 against the dealers 4 thru 6.

This will be expounded upon later, but I just want you to be aware of these things as we go along, so that you'll be ready for them when I go deeper.

As you become more proficient in the count, you'll automatically have a clock turned on in your head that will alert you as to when you've reached the designated areas of 'rich' and 'poor.' Just get turned in on the 'theory' right now.

A) SINGLE DECK
   1) Neutral . . . . 41 to 48
   2) Medium rich . . . . 49 to 53
   3) Medium poor . . . . 36 to 40
   4) Poor . . . . 35 and down
   5) Rich . . . . 54 and up

I think you get the idea. The important part is that you get to understand what you're trying to accomplish. And that is to find that imbalance between the basic ratio of 2¼ small cards to each large card. That's the 3476th times I've said that.

Go back to the example at the beginning of this chapter,

where seven 10 value cards appeared with 4 small ones. Spread the remaining 9 large cards out on a table.

Now apply the remaining 32 small cards and you've got over 3½ small ones for each large one, well above the 2¼-1 ratio. You now have a good reason to adjust your Basic Strategy, knowing the deck is in a 'poor' designation.

If you don't get this point, re-read the chapter.

37

CARD RECOGNITION

Notice that the approach to counting is not based on zeroing in on the value of each card, but merely looking for the difference between it being a ten value card, or non-ten.

If you have to give a different applicable point count to each separate valued card, you'd go buggy-eyed after a couple of shoes.

It is my opinion that this is what drives people away from card counting. The past few years has given me the opportunity of meeting many people involved in gambling. Most of them told me they got away from counting because it was too hard to keep the eyes riveted to the table.

That's because each card had a different amount imposed on it and if you missed a couple, or attached a wrong value, your count would suffer.

It has taken me about ten years to perfect four different methods and believe me, it is hard work. The amount of concentration required is what starts to fray the nerves.

For that reason I decided to concentrate on the system that was the easiest to understand, easiest to use and easiest to pass on to people — like yourself — that will strengthen your game of Blackjack.

From a standpoint of increasing your edge against the house, we are talking about a difference of maybe four tenths of one percent to eight tenths of one percent.

Let's talk rounded off figures. It is possible that the

super advanced complicated application of card counting, based on intricate calculations of exact amounts of count, based on unplayed cards in the shoe, may be more effective. Let's look at the amount of that extra effectiveness.

Admittedly it is better to apply a given number to each card (2 thru 9), in order to arrive at a super accurate analysis, but that's asking a lot of the novice player and occassional player to concentrate on, when it is impossible for them to play every day.

Not everybody can concentrate that long and that good. There are not that many people who play Blackjack every day and there are not that many who will give the time required to perfect that type count.

Kenny Kount can't count the loose change in his pocket. He loves Blackjack and read somewhere that card counting will change his game and make him a winner.

That last sentence is only half right. Card counting will improve your game — but it does NOT guarantee you being a winner.

Only the application of the entire Big 4, primarily Money Management and Discipline will help you win.

Card Counting must be used as I intend it to be. That is to minimize losses by improving your Basic Strategy. And that is the only advantage.

We last left Kenny Kount trying to count out change for his daily stop to get a cup of coffee, cigaretttes and a paper. He finally worked out what the total was. And you want to send this malfunctioning, mathematical moron to a Blackjack table with an advanced card counting method?

But if I could show him a system, whereby all he needed to do is separate the cards into two different sections — high and low, then we've got a chance to reach him.

Alluding back to the advanced card counting method,

giving the player a 2.8% to 3% edge on the house, let's look at my approach.

While it won't be as statistically effective, it will still give a strong indication of the imbalance of small cards to large cards and that is the whole intent. That puts my plus factor at about 1.8% to 2% edge on the house, and that's only a few tenths of a percentage point away.

In my approach to card counting, this system may give away a little bit, but it is simple enough for all the Kenny Kounts to understand and count.

All you need to do is concentrate on ten value cards and non-tens. That is 'card recognition', not separate values per card.

The dealer bangs out a nine, eight, ten, six, seven, four, jack, five, nine and seven. Instead of spinning the wheels of your brain cells and trying to apply different values, you see 8 small cards and 2 large one and immediately arrive at a plus 4.

Heed me, O ye of little faith, this method is a snap er-ooo!

38

RUNNING COUNT

We're still at a one deck game, with a starting count of 45 and a rich point of 49. As we run through the deck, the count will fluxuate either over 45 or under 45, based on how the cards are coming out. That is considered a 'running' count, as the numbers are running all over the place.

At this time I want you to glance over at the used cards and mentally zero in on the approximate amount of cards left in the dealers hand, based on the amount that is already dealt. I touched on this example before and now maybe you can pick up on it a little better.

Kante Weight can't wait for the count to reach a solid plus factor before making a big decision, either knowledge wise or money wise. In the first hand, 7 small cards and one ten is dealt, causing the count to go right up to 50 (rich).

But only 8 cards were dealt during that run and while the balance has shifted, it is much too early to make a monumental move.

By glancing at the discard pile, you can easily see that the deck has hardly even been dented.

At this point I want you to be aware of the running count but hold your britches on. The deck is not in a true rich position. As you get deeper into the deck, maybe approximately halfway, that running count of 50 will pop up and now it means something.

In a one deck game, there is significant impact on the remaining cards and now strong moves could be made.

So don't be a Kante Weight and start mortgaging your

house as soon as the running count climbs a little. Use patience.

Let the running count reach a solidified point and then make your move.

39

TRUE COUNT

True count is a name given to a point in time, in other card counting systems, when the count is absolutely right on the button.

In other words, these systems have a certain number applied to each card and that count is then applied to the exact amount of cards in the discard tray.

But getting this infallible true count takes a lot of practice and an almost fanatical application of precise figures.

You must become a walking computer and cannot afford a blink of a mistake, either keeping your running count up to date, or in sizing up the number of cards left in the shoe.

The result is a tremendously accurate 'True Count' of exactly what cards are left in that playable shoe. But it still treats the two decks that are kept behind the cut card as an average and therein lies the drawback.

In a one deck game where they deal down to the last card, you have the casino backed into a corner. The super advanced system is near foolproof. But here-in lies the drawbacks and I repeat them again...

1) Everyone cannot concentrate this hard,
2) Everyone WON'T concentrate this hard,
3) There are very, very, very few one deck games,
4) In fact, Atlantic City, as of this writing, has only 6 and 8 deck games and an occassional 4 deck one,

5) Vegas has 2 deck games, but some casinos still have cut-offs. So again you can't get down to the actual last card,

6) It takes constant playing — everyday — to stay sharp,

7) There is no room for error and only a tiny percentage of the people reading this page will devote the necessary time.

That brings us back to my system. Maybe you'll give up anywhere from 4 tenths of one percent to one percent by following my advice, but there are a few plus factors:

1) My system is simple,
2) It is easy to learn,
3) It is easy to apply,
4) It is easy to go back to and brush up on,
5) It can be perfected and understood by anyone,
6) You don't have to be a mathematical giant to learn it,
7) Most important...it works!!! What more can you ask?

RUNNING COUNT: Keeps you abreast of the imbalance of just small to large cards, but has a strong effect on improving Basic Strategy.

TRUE COUNT: Takes into consideration the cards dealt, their individual monetary value, and by applying total number of cards remaining in the shoe, gives you an up-to-the-second count (A lot of work).

It is my humble opinion that the 'true count' is too hard on the average player. Many people have told me that they just could not keep sharp long enough to fully concentrate on this method.

My intent is to help you as much as I can, within the guidelines of how much application of my methods I can expect from the majority.

Based on the many hundreds of people I talk to...I can honestly tell you that many, many, many lazy people will not be able to give their full concentration to what's needed.

40

PRACTICE

By now you should be whizzing thru a single deck, counting one card at a time, in 25 seconds or less on a consistent basis. Now we go deeper.

Take the deck and peel off three cards (don't peek) and lay them face down on the table.

Now go through your deck and tell me what those cards are: (small or large).

Let's suppose you complete your deck and end at the following count:

a) 46 . . . . there are 3 small cards
b) 49 . . . . there is one 10 and 2 small
c) 52 . . . . there is one small and 2 tens
d) 55 . . . . there are 3 tens

You can cut a few seconds off your time by three less flips, but the main thing is that the count you end up on, automatically keys what these three face down cards are.

For instance, you end at 49. Two small cards (plus 1) immediately off-set one large card (minus 2). You know right away what those cards are.

Same is when the count ends at 55. It must end at 49, so it takes only a blink to realize that these three cards have to bring you back to 49.

The only thing that will do that is three minus two's (ten value cards), and it pulls your count back to 49.

Okay — go to work on this exercise and it shouldn't take you any time at all to perfect it. It'll chop a few seconds off your time.

41

PRACTICE II

This'll also be a snap, as all we're gonna do it is cut an extra two cards off your start of 52 cards. Place five cards face down on the table and shoot thru your deck. Get final count and name those five cards, as to value.

Here are the possibilities...

a) 44 . . . . there are 5 small cards,
b) 47 . . . . there are 4 small cards and one ten,
c) 50 . . . . there are 3 small cards and two tens,
d) 53 . . . . . . there are 2 small cards and three tens,
e) 56 . . . . there is 1 small card and four tens,
f) 59 . . . . there are five tens.

See how easy it is to glance at these cards and swing back to 49 by adjusting your plus ones and minus twos?

A hint as to how easy it is. Always look to find an offset with three cards. That means two small will offset one large.

Suppose you end at 47. Three of the five cards can be eliminated in a twinkling, by looking to offset their value. Mentally swing three of the cards to the side, knowing that two of them are small and one is large.

That leaves only two cards left and you're still at 47, looking to reach 49. It's pretty obvious those two cards are each plus one, bringing you to the appointed number.

So start practicing this method with five buried cards and again you should pick another second off your time. You should be right around the 20 second mark by now.

The time you take to figure out what those cards are — is not added into your exercise just yet. Eventually I want you to instantly recognize their value, but right now the clock runs only against your going thru the deck.

42

PRACTICE III

Let's step up your drills to a 10 card peel. With the single deck, slide ten cards face down on the table and now proceed counting the remaining deck.

With this many cards on the table, there'll naturally be many more variations. I'm not gonna go into all of them, as by now you're hep on how to use the offset process.

OK, you've finished your count, arrived at 51, and have 10 cards from which to decode. Right off the bat use the offset (2 small to 1 large). That keeps your count at 51, cause you'll use up nine cards. You wanna get to 49, so the last card is a high one.

That means there were six small and four large ones. Now be sure you understand this exercise before moving on. Card counting is an advanced method of speed drills and card recognition.

I'll lay out a few examples to get you going and watch how simple it is to come up with the value of the hidden cards. First use up offsets:

45	2 offsets, plus 4 small,
42	1 offset, plus 7 small,
57	2 offsets, plus 4 large,
48	3 offsets, plus 1 small,
51	3 offsets, plus 1 large.

To repeat: an offset merely means you're trying to nullify a certain amount of cards with a single glance. Two small cards, at plus 1 each, is offset by one large card at minus 2. So try and catch as many offsets as you can.

115

We're getting a little heavy now, so make sure you're staying with us in the manner of perfecting speed.

Don't just practice this a few times and then move to the next chapter. Make sure you're like lightning and that you understand why you're doing this, and what advantage you now have over the dealer, even if we're only at single deck right now.

43

THE OFFSET

I've been talking to you about this move, so now we'll back track and go over it in detail. It is a simple little edge to help you with the speed of counting. Remember what I said about 'card recognition?'

Eventually you will get to a point in counting, whereby just a simple glance across a full table of players will allow you to count every card on that lay-out in a fraction of a second. That is by distinguishing between it being a high or a low card.

Card counting is nothing more than:
1) Speed,
2) Card recognition,
3) Adapting it to your Basic Strategy.

Everything reverts back to speed and the idea is to get you to use short cuts, so as to get you away from staring at the cards for long periods of time.

This offset method allows you to use a three card grouping and offset the necessity of changing your count. As we get deeper into the counting of two and more decks, this three card offset will be used quite extensively, so get accustomed to using it, as I'll keep referring back to it in many instances.

Deal several hands of Blackjack on a table and begin your count at 45. Suppose the dealers up card is a five, and the hand at 1st base is a seven/queen.

Right off the bat you're got an offset: the dealers five and your seven constitute two plus ones. The queen is a minus two. You don't even have to count 46-47-45.

You're gonna end up back at 45 anyway, so just use the two small cards and one large one to offset the chore of counting.

Maybe the hand at position two is a six/eight and the one at third position is a jack/eight.

Take the #2 hand of six and eight, carry over to pick up the jack at #3 hand, use that as an offset, and just add a plus one to your count to cover the eight in hand #3. Now you're at 46 and you've 'offset' seven cards with a mere glance. Work it out — NOW.

The offset is something I have been using for years. At first it will be a little touchy to master, but keep dealing yourself a couple of hands across the table and get in the habit of looking for the plus 1, minus 2 offset.

This is only one of the several different ways to establish a pattern of counting. Each of you will settle on a method that is easy for you, yourself. And that's not wrong.

There is absolutely no set pattern of counting the cards. It comes down to preference of style. You decide the one that is most comfortable.

An upcoming chapter will show variations of counting, but that is only suggested methods. You decide yourself on what fits you best.

The offset can be used in conjunction with other counting systems, so keep it on your back burner.

44

PRACTICE IV—OFFSET

I told you there would be an application of the 'offset,' so I hope you've got the method completely understood.

Right now there's a guy reading this book and his name is Knod N. Agree. As each chapter flips by he reads it, nods that he understands what I'm saying, agrees with my theory, convinces himself that he has practiced it and moves to the next chapter.

Wrong...wrong, a thousand times wrong. Each chapter in itself calls for a period of concentration and practice on that particular part of the method of counting.

I've broken down my method by chapter — to bring you along step-by-step. If this nodding nut Knod is simply going to read words, nod that he understands and moves to the next chapter, the point will come when the only thing he can agree on is that he hasn't the foggiest idea of what I'm talking about.

If you're on the same wave-length as Knod N. Agree, I suggest you back up a few chapters and start doing your homework.

This practice session will only work if you completely understand the previous exercises. Okay, you mastered the art of counting a deck of cards, with ten cards peeled off. You're got your speed down to 19 seconds and can name the value of all ten of those face down cards.

Some of you may be at 18 seconds, while others may be a click or two slower at 21 seconds. It's OK...that speed will improve as your card recognition becomes stronger and stronger.

This exercise is based on one deck, turning over three cards at a time, and naturally starting with a count of 45.

Take a deck, hold it face down and peel off three cards at a time and flip them face up on the table. Use the offset method for this exercise and continue right thru the deck. Just as in the single flip, the count should end at 49.

As you turn three cards at a time on the table, there will be only four possible combinations that could occur:

1) Three small cards,
2) Three large cards,
3) Two small and one large,
4) Two large and one small.

That's the only four combinations that could show, so let's see how that helps our count:

1) Three small cards . . . . plus 3
   a) a snap to remember,
2) Three large cards . . . . minus 6
   a) Again — takes no brains to apply to running count,
3) Two small and one large 0
   a) The offset, which is easiest of all,
4) Two large and one small . . . . minus 3
   a) This is the only fairly difficult one to remember, but it's still in the 'three' family.

Watch how fast you zip thru the deck now. You've reduced your hand flips from 52 to 18, so naturally the required time for this exercise will be lower.

I expect you to do this in 12 seconds. In the beginning you'll slide right down to 16 seconds, and as your card recognition improves, you'll level off at 15 seconds.

The drop to 14 seconds will come as you continue to practice.

This method is the beginning of the application of the three card count, or offset method that I utilize.

Many of you will see the simplicity of it and use it exclusively, or at least a portion of it.

This is a must chapter for swinging into the meat of speed drills. Do not proceed until you master counting a single deck in 15 seconds, over and over and over and over and...

Now comes the necessary off-shoots:

a) Peel one card, lay it face down on table, complete your count and name the value of that card,

b) Peel off 3 cards, and repeat (a),

c) Peel off 5 cards, and repeat (a),

d) Peel off 10 cards and repeat (a),

1) This can be expanded to cover 12, 15, 20 cards pulled from the initial deck. Go ahead and try it.

OK, if you've got this down to a science, your speed should be at 13 seconds, but no more than 14.

Do NOT move on until you've mastered this exercise.

45

READING A HAND

Now that you've mastered the art of counting one deck, three cards at a time, your ability to read cards at a glance should be pretty strong.

The time has come to move that card recognition process over to the table itself. Subsequent chapters will give you a couple of other ways to count, or you may come up with your own method.

But let's start with the offset method and see how you like it, or how well you know it.

To get started, deal out a hand and make believe there are three other players besides yourself and naturally the dealers hand. You are sitting at first base.

As the dealer begins his deal, you concentrate only on your starting number of 45. Do not begin your count until you have both your cards and can see the dealers up card.

Immediately use those three cards to begin your count. Let's say you have a queen/six and dealer has a jack. That comes to a minus 3 and you drop your count to 42.

At this point you haven't even looked at the other players hands. All you should care about is your hand and the dealers up card.

The dealer has completed the deal and now goes right to your hand at first base. You have already counted your queen/six and call for a hit. Each card dealt swings you into your running count.

He gives you a seven and you break. Your count goes to 43 and he takes your hand and places it in the discard container.

Your glance moves to the next hand where the player has a king/four. You have two options at this point.

1) Immediately count those two cards, dropping your count to 42,

2) Wait for the player to take a hit and use the three card offset.

If you have the three card offset down pat, you might like that procedure. If the player does not take a card and waves his hand, you then pick up that minus 1 (in this case) and wait for the dealer to move to the next hand.

Personally, I pick up each players 2 card hand total and immediately add it to my running count. In this case I would drop right to 42 when I saw that king/four (minus 1). The player calls for a hit and gets a three. I count each card separately as it is dealt and now my count is at 43.

The third player has a four/four and you go to 45. He takes a hit, gets a five and you go to 46. Another hit results in a queen and he breaks. Your count drops to 44 and as the dealer snaps up the busted hand, you glance at the last player.

She has a three/jack, which you see as minus one and your count is now 43. A hit pulls a seven and she stops. You're at 44 and the four players hands are completed.

The dealer now moves to his hand — but remember, you already counted his up card of jack, when you added it to your hand.

All you need concentrate on is his hidden card. He exposes an ace and you're at 45. He draws a six and you're at 46. He has a total of seventeen, hand is over.

While he pays the other players, you make a mental note of where you ended (46), and that's where you will begin your count on the next hand.

Just for smiles, go back and reread that example and

then deal it on your table exactly the way it was explained.

In fact, set the cards up to come out exactly the way the example was shown. See if you feel comfortable with this method.

46

SINGLE CARD METHOD

Same amount of people, different system and we'll step up the procedure. Still single deck.

Dealer peels off cards to you and three other players at the table, with you at first base.

Your two cards are seven/eight and the dealer has a six as his up card. Right away you get rid of those three cards by adding a plus 3 to your running count of 45. You get the idea. I use the dealer card to employ my three card offset. My count is 48.

Now it's a snap to revert to a single card for each card that comes out.

Naturally you're standing on your hand of fifteen and now the dealer moves to the second player. As I explained in the previous chapter, you have the option of waiting until this player has three cards to use the offset, or you may count his initial two cards right away and then count each card as it is dealt.

I find the single card method very easy and you beginners might like to use it to get you started.

Player #2 has a five/ace and called for a double down. You jumped your count to 50. and he gets a jack. Your count drops to 48.

Quickly go to player #3 and he has a queen/king. This gives you a minus 4 and running count of 44. He stands.

Player #4 has a queen/deuce, you apply a minus one and drop to 43. She stands with her 12. Dealer turns over his hidden card and it's an ace, giving him a total of 17 (his six was already counted), so you're at 44 and the hand is over.

See how simple that was! I call this method the Single Card System, as you count each card in the players original hand and then adopt a plus one or minus two application as each new card is dealt.

The only time you actually use the three card offset is to cover the dealers up card and the first base players two up cards.

Let's wrap this up by quickly putting this system in order:

    a) Count first base players two cards, with dealers up card,

    b) Count each card dealt separately, as it comes out to that first player,

    c) Count #2 players first two cards and then each of his subsequent hits separately,

    d) Repeat for any additional players,

    e) Wait for dealer to expose hidden card (up card was already counted), and then count subsequent hit on dealers hand.

That's the simple single card and can be used with 1-2-4-6 or 8 decks. Make sure you understand each step, as easy as it may appear.

If fact, deal yourself several hands and practice this method. It may be the one you decide to use.

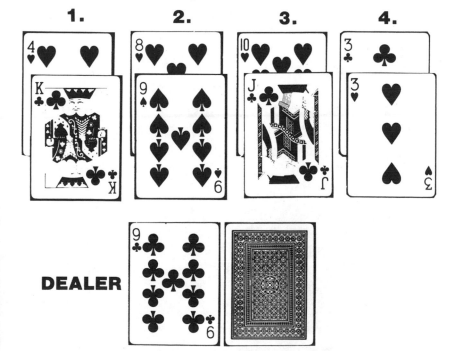

47

STRICTLY OFFSET

By now you know the offset method of looking for 'card recognition' with three cards. A fraction of an instant can tell you if those three cards are plus 3, minus 3, minus 6, or offset.

Since you have practiced the offset count in chapter 32, you should be down to 13 seconds by now. Let's go to a complete offset count, for a hand dealt to these players plus the dealer.

You can deal out a hand, showing the exact cards to coincide with this example:

In this method you'll be counting only by threes, starting with the initial cards that are laid out to begin play.

Starting with a single deck count of 45, take care of your hand and the dealers up card. That means the 4/king of your hand (#1) and the dealers 9 is an offset and you're still at 45.

Immediately swing down the line and combine the hands of the 2nd, 3rd and 4th players:

    a)   8/9 (#2) and 10 (#3) . . . offset, count stays at 45,

    b)   jack (#3) and 3/3 (#4) . . offset, count stays at 45.

Bang!! Just like that you have three sets of offsets and your count is still at 45. Now don't go thinking you can't keep up with the count, as the dealer may go too fast.

He can't go too fast with the offset method. If, and I repeat IF, you have mastered this counting method.

In a glance you have covered hand at first base and dealers up card. As he completes dealing, you pick both cards in hand #2 with large card in hand #3 to make an offset. Then the second card in hand #3 is added to two up cards of hand #4 and you have a quick count.

What you have done is cover the whole board in a twinkling and now you can revert to a single count method as each individual card comes out.

Remember, in this system you are counting the whole layout BEFORE any cards are dealt, other than the initial two up cards for each player and the dealers hand.

OK, your count is still 45 and now the dealer goes around the board:

     . #1) hits, draws a queen (minus 2) . . . . . count at 43,

     #2) stands (no change) . . . . count at 43,

     #3) stands (no change) . . . . count at 43,

     #4) hits, draws a ten (minus 2) . . . . count at 41,

          hits again, draws a jack (minus 2) . . count at 39,

Dealer) turns over a five (plus 1) . . . . . count at 40,
hits, draws a queen (minus 2) . count at 38.

Again hand is completed and you should have zipped thru that exercise.

Without even blinking, fly right into the next chapter, which is another example of the same system. I wanna get your attention while your brain is cooking on this method.

48

EXAMPLE OF OFFSET

Next hand is coming out and you're at 38. It does not matter how many players are competing, as you can combine hands in 3 card offset method, regardless of how many hands there are.

Cards are dealt and they line up:

1. **2.** **3.** **4.**

DEALER

You zip thru offsets, simple as ABC.

    a) #1 hand and dealers up card

        ...plus 3 . . . . count at 41,

b) #2 hand and first card of #3
...offset .count at 41,

c) Second card of #3 and #4 hand
...offset . . . . .count at 41,

Just like that you're at count of 41 and the play now begins:

a) #1 doubles down, draws a six,
(plus 1) .count at 42,

b) #2 splits, draws a ten (minus 2),
has to stand . . . . .count at 40,
second hand of three draws a five
(plus 1) .count at 41,
doubles down, draws a jack
(minus 2), stands . . . . .count at 39,

c) #3 stands (no change) . . . . .count at 39,

d) #4 stands (no change) . . . . .count at 39,

e) Dealer exposes seven (plus 1) . . . . .count at 40,
Dealer draws again, pulls a king
(minus 2), busts . . . . .count at 38,

Work it out yourself using the same cards. If you haven't got this method down pat, you're sorely lacking in the grasp of the offset.

But if you followed this section, chapter by chapter, this method will be like childs play for you.

You may ask: "Why not wait until hand is completely finished and then use strictly offset and take each hand in itself to apply count?"

I'm glad you asked that question. The next chapter answers it. For now, completely understand this method. Again, this may be the one you choose.

Go over some examples and compare it to chapter 34 (Single Card Method). One of these will strike your fancy.

49

VARIATION OF OFFSET

OK, you've mastered the previous chapter and admittedly found it to be very simple. But now you're starting to shift into second gear and find yourself getting faster and faster.

You have the card recognition down to a science and are looking for ways to improve your speed and cut down on the amount of time you have to look at the table.

I'm proud of you...the less time you have to stare at numbers on the cards, the more you prevent drowsiness from becoming an issue.

So you come up with your own theory of the complete offset method. This is how it goes.

You wait until the whole hand is dealt and still you do not make a move to begin your count. Let's suppose you're playing at a table and 45 (for a single deck) is your starting point, as deck is just coming out.

Following hands are laid out:

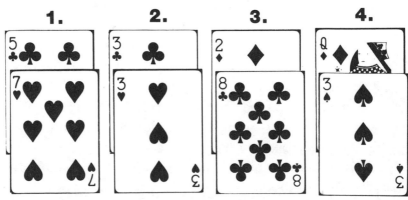

1. **2.** **3.** **4.**

DEALER

Not a move is made. You do not begin your count until dealer completes each separate hand. He begins with player at first base:

Player #1 draws a nine, stands and you now apply the three card count, to give you a plus 3 and count goes to 48.

Dealer moves to #2 player who calls for a hit and draws a deuce, calls for another hit and draws a five and now has 13. He signals again for a hit and draws an ace, giving him 14. Another hit gives him another deuce and now he's at 16. He must draw against dealers ten and calls for a hit. Up pops a queen and hand busts.

Dealer immediately pulls down the hand, before you had a chance to pick up those seven cards. Actually, it came to a plus 4, raising the running count to 52, but before you can back track and concentrate on what those seven cards were, the dealer has now moved to player #3.

There is a tremendous possibility that you will jumble your count at this point and throw off your running total. Naturally you must abandon your count for this deck. You lose the chance of utilizing a rich deck.

And all because too many cards were used in a particular hand and immediately pulled away by the dealer.

Hand #3 comes out and player quickly pulls a four, then an ace, then a king, giving him a busted hand and a run of 2-8-4-ace-king.

Again the dealer slides the hand away before you have zeroed in on that overall plus 2. Your count should be at 54, but you're all confused.

You spend so much time trying to re-picture the two previous hands, you missed the nine that was dealt to player number 4. All you see is the dealer pulling another busted hand away and couldn't tell if the draw card was an eight, a nine or a ten. Actually, the count is 54, but you're in never-never land and not aware of it.

Dealer reveals his hole card of five and draws a five, giving him a total of twenty and keeping the deck at a rich 54.

By rights, the next hand should treat the deck as 'rich,' to take advantage of the plus in tens still remaining. But that little detour back in hand #2 has thrown you off kilter and all you can do is approach the upcoming hand as a neutral count.

Now look at the mess you're in. If you're dealt a 16 vs the dealers up-card of seven, the proper move would be to stand — since the deck is rich. But you don't know it's rich, as you've lost count and must treat the play as a neutral move.

You call for a hit and grab a jack, killing your hand. One slip and you cost yourself money.

I do not like this variation, for the reason stated above. Now you can agree with my thoughts on it, or find a way to deal with it. I'd rather see you begin to count as soon as you see hand at first base and dealers up card.

50

LAS VEGAS METHOD

By now you should have decided on which system of counting you will use. You'll notice that the examples I've shown is applicable only where the players two cards are exposed — as in Atlantic City.

But suppose you're engaged in a Blackjack game where the players cards are dealt face down. You have no way of counting these cards, unless the player shows his hand at the end of play.

This is a snap when he doesn't break, since he must show the dealer his hand, in order to collect his winning bet.

But the play in Vegas and in many other casinos around the world call for the players first two cards to be dealt face down.

When you wish to draw a card, you make a sweeping move with your hand of cards, to indicate to the dealer you wish a card. He then deals your card face up on the table and any subsequent cards you may wish to pull.

In some casinos they deal the cards you draw face down. When that particular player busts he may just toss his hand, still face down, to the dealer who buries the cards. You never get to count their value.

Naturally if you're counting, you gotta see each card. With this method of dealing, where you don't see every card, counting is impossible, hopeless, futile. Take your choice or take all three.

Years ago I was in a game out west — counting against

the single deck they were using and doing quite well. The pit boss realized I was counting and sent in a shill to "hide" some cards. What he'd do was call for a hit and then another and then toss his hand face down to the dealer, depriving me of the chance to count.

It took me only to the second hand to realize I was discovered as a counter. The shill (who works for the house) was dealt two cards face down and signalled for a hit — then another hit, then another.

He studied his 5 card hand very intently, looked over at me and signalled for another hit and then another. That gave him seven cards and me an idea that something didn't smell two sweet.

He was calling for his eighth card as I slid off my stool. Then he stopped and threw his cards to the dealer, who moved over to my hand, which I completed and then left the table.

As I walked away from the table, I gave a look at the sharp pit boss. He gave me a look that indicated that he knew that I knew, that he knew, that I knew that he knew, that I knew...

Card counting works only in games where you can see every card.

51

RICH AND RICHER

Still with one deck, let's look at how you will qualify a deck as to reaching a true 'rich' count. This was touched on in chapter 20, but it's worth another pop.

When your count hits 49, regardless of the number of decks that are used, you reach a classification of 'rich' because we've used up those four extra cards per deck.

Suppose a deck begins and you get a nine/eight and the dealer draws an ace/eight on his two cards. The hand is over and four non-tens were dealt, raising the count to 49. There are 32 remaining small cards and 16 large. Ratio is at 2-1 and we have a 'rich' count. But it came too fast to have a big impact.

The higher the count, the richer the remaining deck or shoe becomes. Following table defines the various points:

    a) 41 to 48 . . . . Neutral,
    b) 49 to 56 . . . . Rich,
    c) 57 to 63 . . . . Very rich,
    d) 64 and up . . . . Very, very rich.

If you're playing at a table where your count is 64 or higher, you better believe there is a bevy of ten value cards in your future. You sure as heck better be adjusting your basic strategy to take advantage of that swing.

There are different levels of 'rich' and that will also tie in with the remaining cards in the shoe. That'll be touched on shortly, but for now get to understand the different classifications of richness.

52

POOR, POORER

Just as important as the rich and richer deck, is the poor, poorer one. You can do just as much to improve your basic strategy with a poor deck, as you can with a rich one. This was covered in Chapter 21.

With 'neutral' starting at 45 and going up thru 48, it also swings down to a count of 41, while retaining the designation of 'neutral.'

As the large cards continue to come out, the count will keep dropping. In between 36 and 40 I call it 'medium poor.' That means the tens are disappearing and the ratio of small cards to large is climbing.

Here again it behooves you to keep an eye on the discard tray, to help you to gauge just how rich or poor the remaining cards are — based on a logical application of starting decks, minus cards in discard tray.

Use this guide:

    a) 41 to 48 . . . . Neutral,
    b) 36 to 40 . . . . Medium poor,
    c) 30 to 35 . . . . Poor,
    d) 29 and down . . . . Very poor.

Look how powerful your moves can be if you reach that very poor classification, especially when you're dealt 12's, 13's and 14's. We'll go deeper into this later, but it's obvious how you can adjust your basic strategy to coincide with this running count that is dropping, indicating a predominance of non-tens remaining in the shoe.

Those last two chapters are intentional repeats of #20

and #21, even though it touches on a boring message. At least you've got it banged into your head that 41 to 48 is 'neutral' and 40 and lower swings into the 'poor' class.

53

WRAPPING UP ONE DECK

We're at the end of the application of the count — as applied to one deck. We'll be moving to the multiple decks now, but first let's be sure you're on the right wave length.

You know by now that counting is absolutely nothing more than card recognition and speed. The use of multiple decks by the casino, is to offset the power of the card counter, so all we do is change our starting figure to readjust ourselves to the number of decks they use.

So far, during this section of the book called "Knowledge of the Game," we've talked only about single decks. Here are the highlights:

1) **52 cards** in a deck, 16 tens, 36 non-tens,
2) **Ratio** of small to large cards is 2¼ to 1,
3) **Theory** of card counting is that deck is in favor of the player when ratio of small cards to large is better than 2¼ to 1,
   a) Example: Half the deck is completed and 26 cards are dealt. Of the 26 remaining cards, 14 are small and 12 are large. Ratio is only 7 to 6. Deck is rich in tens.
4) **'Rich' designation:** means remaining cards in deck or shoe is rich in tens, in relation to non-tens, better than 2¼ to 1.
5) **'Poor' designation:** means remaining cards in deck or shoe is poor in tens, even worse than

2¼ to 1 ratio. Could be 3-1 or 4-1 or even 5-1.

6) **Application of count:** Every ten value card is minus 2. Every non-ten is plus 1.

7) **Single deck count:** begins at 45.

8) **When count reaches 49:** deck is 'rich' because now ratio is less than 2¼ to 1.

9) **Speed and card recognition:** only requirements of counting.

10) **Speed:** Getting your count down to at least 14 seconds per deck, 13 seconds is excellent, 12 is perfect. (That's all I'll accept.)

11) **Card recognition:** Being aware of the value of a card or group of cards, in a fraction of a second.

12) **Offset:** A method of counting 3 cards at a time — using values of highs and lows to offset each other.

13) **Running count:** Practice of keeping an accurate numbered total of the deck or shoe. Count begins when deck comes out with opening hand and is completed when dealer reshuffles.

14) **Buried cards:** Casinos will 'bury' approximately 2 decks to try and negate the power of the counter.

15) **Single Card Method:** Counting each card individually, as it is dealt.

16) **Offset Method:** Counting the cards in groups of three, on initial two card hands, and then reverting to single card count as each player makes his decisions as to hit, stand, split or double.

Memorize all of the above and if anything isn't clear, revert back to that chapter. By this time I expect you to:

    a) Have single deck count, with three card off-set, at 13 seconds and be able to identify value of 10 peeled off cards.

    b) Decide on whether you will use Single Card Count or Offset Method.

Decide right now...

54

DISCARD TRAY

When dealer clears the cards off a table after player breaks, or when the hand is completed, he'll place them in a plastic holder to his right.

It is called a discard tray and is easily visible to everyone at that table. A lot of card counters keep their eyes glued there.

If you're a veteran card player, regardless of what game you're playing, you can look at a stack of cards and ascertain the approximate number of cards in that pile.

I want you to keep an eye on that discard tray and become adept at telling how many decks or half decks are in that tray.

If you're playing at a table, ask the dealer how many decks he is using. Usually it'll be 6 or 8. Sometimes you'll find a four deck game in Atlantic City.

In a six or eight deck game, they will cut off about two decks, so you know how many decks remain to be used.

Start practicing your ability to guess the number of cards in a pile. Lay out different heights of cards, guess the number of decks and half decks. Then count those piles to see how close you came.

With a lot of practice, you should be able to come within six cards of what is actually in that discard tray.

This is a simple exercise and the next chapter will show you how to take advantage of this Knowledge.

55

REMAINING DECKS

The previous chapter covered the discard tray and now we get to see where it can be used in our play.

Let's say the house is using a 6 deck game. You've been counting for several hands and reach a count of 54, so you know the shoe is rich.

Based on the fact that two decks are cut off in that six deck shoe, you know you're dealing with a four deck game — using the two decks you'll never see as neutral. This is the only way we can offset those two decks. You can't see them, so treat them as if they don't exist — cause as far as you're concerned, they don't.

By checking out the discard tray, you can tell how many decks, or at least approximately how many decks have been used. If one deck has been used, it means there are three remaining decks and the rich count of 54, while it is accurate, is somewhat watered down, so to speak.

I still treat it as a rich deck, but as you'll see in the Money Management section, I tread softly on the variations of bets I will apply, cause only one deck was used.

However, if I reach a count of 54, check out the discard tray and find that three decks were stacked there, it puts a little different light on my knowledge.

Now there is only one deck left to come out and that is a 'true', powerful, rich deck about to be dealt.

Get in the habit of checking that discard tray when your count reaches either a 'poor' or 'rich' designation. See how many decks are still to be played before the cut card appears.

The more cards in that discard tray, the less to be dealt and the more true that count will be.

Tie these last two chapters together, put their message on your back-burner and keep it ready to bring forward when you start your play.

56

2-4-6-8 DECKS

It's not hard to get me mad at a lecture or seminar. Just ask me a silly question, or make a stupid remark, and it touches my boiling point. I don't wanna see anyone gamble unless they're perfect and if they do risk their money on games they know little about, I think they're jerks. And it's no problem to tell them so.

When we get to talking Blackjack and card counting at a lecture, invariably someone will make the statement: "Ah, you can't count with six and eight decks." Who is this excuse for an expert trying to kid? He shows his lack of smarts by making that idiotic statement.

Of course you can count cards when they use multiple decks and, yes, there will be a marked improvement in your play if you're a perfect counter. You must utilize the running count to improve your play. It alerts you to all imbalances in the remaining shoe.

Sometimes to make a point, I'll ask someone how many tens and how many non-tens there are in a single deck. A lot of times the ridiculous retort is that: "Yeah, but they use eight decks."

It doesn't matter if they use 467 decks, the ratio of small cards to large cards is always the same. If the house did not fear the counter, they wouldn't go to all the trouble of using multiple decks.

Naturally you get a truer picture of the amount of large card impact when they use one deck, but that's a difficult game to find in the casinos nowadays.

When they went to two decks, we just changed our starting number. When they added two extra decks and went to four, we did the same thing. It climbed to six and eight decks and the card counter merely adjusted the number he used to begin the count — when the shoe first came out.

This will be covered in the next three chapters, but wanna get that gobbily garbage out of your head.

    a) Counting against one deck is like having a license to steal,

    b) Counting against two decks is almost as good, but you have a club instead of a gun,

    c) Four decks is a pretty decent game and you get a lot of strong true counts,

    d) Six decks start to get tough, but you still will find the imbalance popping up,

    e) Eight decks is about the same as six. It's tough, but still effective to the player.

Bottom line is that card counting is a tool that can be used to improve your game. So look away when you get illogical advice from people who don't know what they're saying.

You got two choices, even with six and eight deck games:

    1) Don't play Blackjack,

    2) Play Blackjack if you have a card counting method with side count of aces.

If you're a non-believer or skeptic, close the book right now, as you're really not believing what you're reading anyhow.

But if you can accept the fact that counting will give you an edge of 2% over the house — as little as that may sound to you — read on!

57

STARTING COUNT

By now you know the Theory of counting, as looked upon by the professional player. The richer the shoe, with a small amount of cards to be played, the better to take advantage of that knowledge.

With one deck I start my count at 45 and, of course, you can start there or pick any number you want. Set your rich point only 4 ticks away from that starting count, in order to pick up those four extra small cards per deck.

But stay a long ways from zero, cause you don't want to get all confused with plus and minus. Better you just stay with the numbers I give you.

For the novice, I'm trying to apply as little pressure or thought processes to your counting as I can. You mathematical geniuses, that are eons of years ahead of us plodding arithmetic nomads, can come up with your own starting figures.

A quick reminder of the starting point for the various decks, in case you forgot:

One deck 45
Two decks 41
Three decks 37
Four decks 33
Five decks 29
Six decks 25
Seven decks 21
Eight decks 17

On the situation of the eight decks, since you're so

close to zero, it's permissible to make a little change. Add ten to your count of 17 and start at 27. Then add ten to your rich count of 49 and get rich at 59. It's just a little hedge against the chance of getting down to zero. But don't lose sight of the fact that your rich point has changed.

Be sure you understand the reasoning behind the dropping of the starting count. Each deck has 36 small cards to 16 large and the counter must use up those extra cards to drop his ratio to 2-1.

Since 45 was our starting mark for one deck and 49 is 'rich,' we are chopping away at those four extra cards. When it is a two deck game, there are four more small cards that have to be disposed of, so our starting count drops to 41.

Now we're trying to use up eight cards before we get to 49. It's a tick harder to reach the 49, but still a great opportunity when you only have to buck two decks.

58

BURIED CARD

Anyone who has played Blackjack in a casino is aware that the dealer always buries the first card out of the shoe.

I can tell you eyeball to eyeball that I cannot give you an intelligent reason why they do it. It surely isn't intended to throw a monkey wrench into the counting pattern of the advanced player, for one logical reason.

The dealer shuffles the cards and buries 'approximately' two decks, based on the mark on the side of the shoe, that indicates where two decks would be.

Since we consider those two decks as neutral, what's so difficult about accepting that one buried card that the dealer slides out of the shoe as also being part of those two decks?

That's what I do. I just figure that one last card didn't make it into the two buried decks so I completely put it out of my mind and don't even worry about what it is.

Kenni Cee is a little paranoid about that card. You've probably seen him at a Blackjack table. As soon as the dealer slides that first card out of the shoe and buries it in the discard tray, poor Kenni starts sweating.

He's taken a 6 month correspondence course in card counting and thinks that he must know what the first card was.

Oh, he has no trouble accepting a neutral count for the two buried decks, but that extra card has already caused him to go gray at the temples and he's only twenty-six.

If the value of that card is so important to you, there are

150

two options:

> 1) Consider it as part of the two buried decks (forget it),
> 2) Ask to see the card.

Holy mackeral Andy, Kenni Cee just sprouted eight more gray hairs. He doesn't want to blow his cover as a counter.

Get off that ego trip. If you can't add that extra card to the two buried decks, ask to see it. Nothing will happen to you. Ninety five percent of the time the dealer will gladly show it to you.

When it happens, Kenni Cee usually strains a groin muscle patting himself on the back. He thinks everybody at the table now knows he's a counter and he secretly loves the sideway glances that some people give him.

Usually this guy can't count to 23, but he wants people to think he's got his head in the game.

Then he'll make eleven consecutive mistakes in basic strategy.

Personally, I don't ask to see the buried card and simply consider it part of the two cut decks.

Use your own discretion, but I'd love to see you slide over to a more relaxed and ego-less way of gambling. Don't be looking to be noticed at the table.

59

PRACTICE—AGAIN

Don't think I forgot to put you through a practice run. You're long overdue.

In this one I'd like you to take six decks, start your count at 25, bury 20 cards, and go thru the usual ritual.

Based on 13 seconds for one deck, I'd like your speed for six decks, minus those 20 buried cards, to be no more than one and a half minutes.

Now don't go getting all bent out of shape by that figure. Ninety seconds is time enough for you to apply card recognition and speed to something that should be second nature for you by now.

If it takes you two minutes and you can accurately give the value of those two cards, that is fair. But don't consider that as being a good counter. That means you are only fair and totally unacceptable — as far as I'm concerned.

Keep working on your speed until you've got it down to 90-95 seconds and then accurately naming those 20 buried cards.

When you have completed the practice time for this chapter, you can consider yourself in line with the speed requirements.

Don't forget, you still have to apply the correct strategy moves to your game, so speed is not the only essential ingredient. But it is a big step.

Let me pop a word in about jumping to a six deck drill. I'm very aware that we skipped over the four deck exercise. It's just that I wanna get you banging away at a larger game.

If any of you wish to practice against four decks, go right ahead. Bury 20 cards and start your count at thirty three. This drill should be completed in one minute. If you've conquered the two deck drill, this'll be a snaperoo.

Then move right into the six deck speed counting drills.

60

BACK COUNTING

Maybe you're heard the term before, but I have my own explanation for this phrase. Many card counters will not play in a game until they find the count to be favorable. That means they will not jump into a game when the shoe is first coming out. I've already discussed how to chart a table, but this comes into conjunction with charting a game.

It calls for you to wait until a dealer shuffles all the cards in a shoe and readies the table for a whole new come-out.

The counter will stand off to the side and begin his count. He does not sit at the table. He'll keep an eye on the discard tray as the hands continue to come out and naturally it's very easy for him to merely keep his running count and side count of aces.

When the count reaches the rich key of 49, he buys in and is already aware of the status of the shoe. There are different theories that the various back counting card counters will employ. They all have a certain point at which time they will get involved. Naturally no theory is wrong, but let's take a look at the different points of entry:

1) Wait for running count to reach 49,
2) Wait for running count to reach 'approximately' 49,
3) Wait for running count to drop to 10 and buy in (poor count),
4) If count stays neutral, they may let whole shoe pass without playing,

5) If combination of poor running count and strong dealer up-cards prevail, some counters will move on to other tables.

Don't just let the rich or poor designation prevail. Watch that dealers up-card.

I think you get an idea of what a lot of strong counters will do. Each of these theories are effective, depending upon the outlook of that particular counter. And they're all self explanatory. Match the reasoning with the different theories. See above:

1) This person will play only when that deck is rich,

2) This counter waits until the running count passes the neutral stage and gets to around 40-43,

3) This counter waits for the rich deck, but also will jump in — if the count drops to 10 or less,

4) This is a situation where the counter may get stuck back-counting a table, where the shoe stays neutral. The ones with strong discipline will not buy in. They may even wait only two shoes and then move on,

5) This counter may see that the dealer is turning over power cards and not even bother to wait for a rich count. He goes to another table.

These are all traits that are followed by different counters and naturally there are many, many more. Maybe you'll even invent some of your own.

It's all in how you personally set up your approach.

Last but not least, is the counter who waits only for a rich count but does not settle into that game. He'll make one or several bets at the table, as long as the deck stays rich and then move on.

Since you've taken the time to concentrate on counting, it's only right to assume that you will come up with your own theory of play. For that reason I'd like you to just think for a second about the two most prominent types of counters:

1) The player who comes into a game and bets small until the shoe becomes rich. He'll stay at that table, shoe after shoe.

2) The hit and run counter who back counts, waits for a rich shoe and then makes several bets and goes to another table.

Neither of these types are wrong. Number two takes a fantabulous amount of discipline and is rarely used by more than a handful of players. Yet it is a very powerful approach.

Then we have theory number one, which most of you will follow. In fact, this is the most widely used method, since most players want to settle into a seat and not move.

Neither system is wrong, but I give a lot of credit to the counter who can exhibit the self control it takes to wait and wait and wait and wait and wait for only a rich count to appear before making his wagers. That's Discipline and I love it.

Sometimes it will take hours to reach this point, especially in six and eight deck games. If this is the way you can get yourself to play, you'll find yourself playing only when you've got counts of 49 or higher.

61

FIRST BASE

I'd like to put to bed a myth about card counting in general and Blackjack in particular. The player at 3rd base does not determine the outcome of the game. An upcoming chapter goes into that.

My intention is to make you aware of the right place to sit at a table if you are a counter. That spot is first base and again it comes down to a logical reason.

Let's say there are seven players at the table and the count has reached 54. Now we've got a rich count and the counter wants to take advantage of it.

If he is sitting at first base, he'll get the first card and the ninth card out of the shoe.

The player at third base gets the seventh and the 15th. By the time his hand is completed, there is the chance that the deck might turn back to neutral.

If I'm gonna go to all the trouble of becoming a card counter, I want everything working for me.

One of those things is sitting at first base and taking advantage of the richness of that deck or shoe. This is especially true in a one or two deck game, where the count can fluxuate so quickly.

Even in a six or eight deck game sit at first base. I'm not giving you options on this advice. Strictly first base!!!

Wait a minute — I'll relent and give you the option where to sit:

1) On your dumper,
2) On your left ear.

...As long as it is first base (the first seat at the table).

So if first base ain't open at the table you're charting and back counting at, don't waste your time. Find a table where first base is open and start your charting, only where you have the chance to enter the game at that seat.

Man, I hope none of you cats took the option of sitting on your left ear. Now you can't hear what I'm saying...

62

THIRD BASE

I've already touched on this. It's unbelievable the number of people who honestly think that the person sitting at third base actually determines whether the whole table wins or loses.

That's a lot of hogwash. It just happens that the last move you remember is the person at third base.

There are decisions made all around the table that affect the card the dealer will eventually pull and none are less or more important than the other.

Even if there was a rotten player at third base who continually made stupid moves, in the long run his moves would have a way of evening out.

You just tend to remember the ones that cost you a hand.

I love to watch Iff Heeda at a table. After a hand is over, wherein some guy makes a move that hurts the whole table, this mathematical defunct goes into his act. He starts going over each hand, one by one, and yelling "if he had stayed, she gets that card and if she had hit, you'd get that card and then you would have hit and caught that card, if only he had hit when I wanted him to...

On and on he goes, reliving each move that would have happened, if only he or she had done such and such a thing.

Of all the gobbley garbage, the Iff Heeda's at a Blackjack table rank right up there with the dopiest.

Three hands later, Iff Heeda is still dying about a past

hand. It never ends until he wins a hand when somebody else shoulda, or coulda or woulda done something other that he dida.

If the other players at a table bother you, do the following:

    a) Don't pay attention to them,

    b) Leave the table.

Do you think you're gonna find perfect players at another table???

Dream on!! And who the deuce are these characters who usually cry the loudest? Usually a guy who makes a bushel of mistakes himself, but doesn't even realize it.

Stop your belly-aching, or play a game where the other players don't make decisions, like Baccarat or Roulette.

63

SIDE COUNT OF ACES

The most powerful card in the deck is the ace — cause it can be used as one or eleven. Secretly, everyone hopes for the ace to pop up in their hands, and rightfully so.

Put an ace in every hand you play during a session of Blackjack and it would be odds on that you'd win money that day.

OK, so if it's such a powerful card, why not keep a running count on just how many aces are left in the shoe. There are two different methods for counting aces, to coincide with the number of players at a table:

    a) Full table of seven players,

    b) Two or three players at a table.

Start with a full table of seven players, plus the dealer. To complete a hand of Blackjack it takes an average of 3½ cards per hand. With a full table, you have eight hands being dealt, giving you approximately 28 cards being used. That's a half deck.

Since a half deck constitutes 26 cards, you are safe to figure that in that particular hand you should have seen two aces pop up.

In two hands there should have been four aces coming out of that shoe — because there are four aces in a deck and two hands will give you approximately a full deck being used — when seven players are in action.

I'm looking to see when that shoe shows an imbalance of aces, either from the plus or minus side. So when I play at a full table, or back count from a standing position, it is very easy to keep a side count of aces.

Take a handful of red and white chips that act as your counter. When a hand is started, place a red chip to the side to indicate a half deck. Each time an ace shows, add a white chip. If the laws of probability fall as they should, there would be two white chips for every red one.

Suppose three hands are dealt, giving you 3 red chips off to the side. And suppose in those three hands only 2 aces showed (2 white chips). There should have been six.

That means there are four extra aces banging around in that shoe. Your chances of getting Blackjack has increased because of those extra aces. So has your chances of using an ace to double down or to split.

In other words, the chances of getting more money against the dealer has taken a turn in your favor. The Money Management section covers my betting increases in this situation, so I won't go into that right now. But you can see how good it is to know when there are extra aces in that shoe.

OK, now go to the other side of the coin. Three hands are dealt, cause you have three red chips in that pile. Six white chips should be there.

But alas and alack, there are 11 white ones in that group. That means five extra aces slid out of that shoe. I'd like to slide off my stool.

The chances of getting aces has declined, along with your chances of getting Blackjack. Also your double down opportunities with ace/two, ace/three, ace/four, etc.

Naturally the betting on subsequent hands will decrease and this'll be banged around later, but dwell on these situations for a second. Who the heck wants to play at a game where the chances to get powerful hands has been so curtailed?

Counting aces is an easy thing to do and the information has a dual purpose:

1) You know when your chances of getting an ace has increased,

2) You know when your fighting a shoe with a shortage of those aces.

Give a look. You're sitting in a six deck game and your running count has reached 16, indicating the shoe is poor in tens.

Your side count of aces indicates a negative 5, based on the decks that have been used and there are only two playable decks left in the shoe.

Hey, baby, even Daffy Duck would realize he's in hot water. Options are to bet the smallest amount possible or leave that table. Do you have the guts to leave that table with the odds stacked very, very high against you??? I wonder...

The next chapter goes over another method of side counting aces.

64

VARIATIONS OF SIDE COUNT

Here is how I'd like you to count the aces when there are less than seven players at a table. Continue to let a red chip indicate a half deck and the white ones will indicate an ace.

When the shoe comes out and the first hand is being dealt, do not put a red chip to the side, since a half deck will not be used for only 2 or 3 players at a table. If any aces show, do the same thing as the previous chapter indicated. Every ace calls for you to place a white chip in a separate pile.

With this method, it is necessary that you keep an eye on the discard tray. Wait until a full deck has been used and then slide two red chips into that pile. By now you should be able to tell when there are about 52 cards in a stack.

Suppose you're playing with one other player at a table and during the course of the previous six hands, you saw 10 aces show. That means you would have ten white chips in your 'side' pile.

As soon as you see that a full deck has been reached (a red chip is used for each half deck), slide two red ones into that pile. Now start your offset move so that you don't get too big a pile.

Since each red chip indicates a half deck and each white one stands for an ace, simply remove the two red chips and four white ones and you're left with six white chips. That remaining shoe is way, way down in aces and the chances of winning at that table is in a rotten position. Personally, I'd leave.

See how easy it is to keep these side counts? One thing to keep in mind. Let the red chip indicate a half deck, as you want to stay as accurate as possible with your running count and keeping track down to a half deck is important.

A final word on this move. I've explained how powerful those aces are and you're probably already aware of it. A shoe that is devoid of aces can ruin your game. You've lost many split, doubling and Blackjack possibilities.

But when your count indicates there are a lot of aces left — attack that shoe.

65

OTHER SIDE COUNTS

You've undoubtedly heard of card counting systems that call for you to keep side counts of fives, deuces, and how many times a person sneezed at your table.

Only one of those side counts has any real value. The guy that's sneezing may have pneumonia, so use blue chips to count his sneezes. When your count reaches 43 leave that table, regardless of how many decks have been used.

Other than that, I disagree with any other side counts. Sure there are arguments pro and con for keeping these extra counts, but I believe it is too confusing for the amount of benefit you would gain.

One of the biggest extra side counts is the one on the five. I do not keep track of the fives, so I won't tell you to do it.

I believe that if the five is so important, then the four is in the same family and the next thing they'll want you to count is blinks, burps or coughs.

The counting of aces is mandatory for being a great counter and if I were to keep another side count, it would be the nines. Those things scare me almost as much as the tens and aces.

Just don't go overboard about side counts. The aces are enough.

66

USING THE RICH COUNT

Slowly we creep towards the final use of the count. There are several theories about how to use the Knowledge of the count, whether 'rich' or 'poor,' and each has it's own value.

My use of the count may vary with other opinions, but I honestly don't give a rat's tail what folk lore has been passed on by the hordes of 'experts.'

My Theory on gambling is different than most others. It is very, very conservative. But it works and I hope you'll give it a long look and a long, long try. It's a snap to understand and just as easy to apply. Just ride along these last few pages of suggestions. Think you'll catch the idea very easily.

First take the theory that mostly pops up from other sources:

    a) When the deck becomes rich, increase your bet by four or six or eight units.

      1) That's because the deck is rich in tens and in favor of the player.

NO, NO, NO, a thousand times NO. I agree the player now knows the imbalance of the shoe, but I do not agree with increasing your bet this much, even though the deck has become rich in tens. This is my Theory:

    a) Use your awareness of the richness or poorness of a deck to improve your basic strategy.

It has been accepted by every professional Blackjack player in captivity, that basic strategy and it's variations is the proper way to insure making the best percentage moves of hit, stand, split or double.

Basic Strategy keeps the strong player alive and always will. Then let's use this extra knowledge of 'rich' and 'poor' to further improve that strategy.

In the Money Management section you will be shown how to bet, so keep your socks on and we'll get to that part. But realize what you want to accomplish when you get a strong counting point of 6 (very poor) or 65 (very rich). Me? I use it to make powerful strategic decisions.

That's the way I'd like to see you play. This improvement in your basic strategy is the main use for the running count and will do wonders for your game.

67

VARIATIONS IN BASIC STRATEGY

In the beginning of the book you saw my Basic Strategy chart and by now I expect you to know it inside out, backwards and forwards.

And now that you do, you'll be required to make instant adjustments to that chart, based on the running count. Let's start with the easiest example I can think of: the breaking hand vs the dealer's up card.

If every person playing Blackjack in a casino, would conform to this basic rule, the intelligence level of all players would shoot sharply skyward. This is the biggest mistake of most Blackjack players:

    a) They will NOT hit the breaking hand against that dealers standing hand of 7 thru ace.

That simple move is killing more players than any other standard move. When you have 12, 13, 14, 15, or 16 you MUST hit. Since the average player is not a counter, they have to look at every deck or shoe as if it were neutral.

Then comes the counter and his logical approach to the game, based on his running count. He knows exactly when an imbalance will set in.

The count climbs to 57, only about two decks left in the shoe and you're dealt a ten/four. That deck is rich and you're likely to catch a ten.

You now adjust your strategy and stand with that fourteen. That's because your chances of breaking has increased, due to the richness of that deck or shoe. Why hit into a rich shoe, where you have a strong possibility of getting whacked with a ten?

That's the single most powerful adjustment in strategy and this move alone will save you countless losses, when you perfect counting.

There's a Basic Strategy variation chart that covers these moves. Skip ahead a couple of pages and take a quick gander at it. Go down to where the players hand is a fourteen vs the dealers 7 through ace. Normal strategy says hit.

Keep sliding across the page to where it indicates the count is 52 or higher. The decision is to now stand. That's because the shoe is rich and chances have swung over to the possibility that you'll catch a ten and break. You don't have to be a genius to realize you should back off and stand with that breaking hand.

This is the edge the counter has and it is basically my own personal reason for counting. It's a tremendous tool in the hands of a sharp player.

As you drift through the upcoming chapters, I'd like you to see what I'm trying to get across. When that deck reaches a strong determination of rich or poor you immediately zero in on the adjustments to your play.

This is not hard to do, but you must WANT to be a winner. I can teach you how to win, but each one of you must have it banged into your head that it is the only purpose for your gambling. To win...

As Irene Cara tells you: "What a Feeling!!!"

68

VARIATION CHART

The previous chapter covered my Theory on how to use the count. Now you'll see a detailed chart showing you how to apply these various moves. Do you have to memorize this chart? Yes! Is it easy to memorize? Yes!

First of all, you have to be perfectly aware of each move. Oh, there'll be instances where you can cheat a number or two with no appreciable damage to your overall play, but it is imperative that you see what I'm trying to explain.

Secondly, it will be a snap to memorize, because the logic of these moves are so apparent, that you probably already know them without getting too deep into the chart:

1) When deck is rich, stand with breaking hands vs dealers standing card,

2) When deck is poor, hit your 12, 13, 14 vs the dealers two or three.

The logic behind these moves is so easy to digest, that this should be simply automatic for you. Look at (2) above.

You're playing in a six deck game where the count has dipped to 9. You're dealt a five/eight vs the dealers four.

Your chances of catching a ten value card has diminished, especially if you're deep into the shoe and so you may as well take the hit. In the same vein, you don't want to give that dealer the opportunity to pull into a poor count, when he is sitting with a four. No matter what he shows as his buried card, his chances of breaking are small, so you gotta puff up your hand anyway. Half the so-called genuises at that table will give you dirty looks, but ignore them. Logically, you gotta improve your sloppy 12 thru 14 when that deck is poor.

See how simple this is? In fact, you'll probably sit down and write a sequel to my book and cover the same theory. Like I've said, counting is all logic and speed. Winning is all Money Management and Discipline.

Take a look at the chart in the next chapter that shows the variations that you will use, based on the fluxuation of the count. A few paragraphs ago I told you that it wouldn't be disastrous to be off a tick on some of these moves. For example, take your hand of 16 and the dealer is showing an eight. Basic strategy says to hit, but the count is 49, so the variation is to stand. Go a step further. Suppose the count is 47, same cards but there is only a deck left in the shoe. In that case I would stand at 47 and even 45. That's a true count and I don't wanna hit into a deck approaching a 'rich' point. Especially with only a half deck left to play.

Now...read that previous chapter over and over and over again. Not particularly for that specific example, but to understand the multiple amount of variations that will occur. And I am talking about hundreds of them. In fact, the one I showed you could have variables based on the running count and the amount of decks left in that shoe, either very few or a lot.

It would be absolutely impossible to list every single variation, but I've given you the key number to use for a card counting move. Once you memorize the chart and the count that calls for a move, you can use your own opinion or theory as to when to deviate.   Look how far you've come in the book. I've been showing you the Theory of counting and how to arrive at such a point.

Well, this chapter shows you what to do when you get there. The chart in the next chapter should become your bible of moves. After you master the moves, make your own adjustments, according to how comfortable you feel making such a move.

One more note. Even if this chart looks too long to memorize, it isn't. And as you get stronger, you'll make moves by INSTINCT at the table. Don't laugh, that's exactly what will happen. You'll become so good at knowing what cards will come out of the shoe, you'll think you can read into the future.

69

VARIATIONS OF BASIC STRATEGY

YOUR HAND	DEALER'S UP CARD	BASIC STRATEGY	COUNT	DECISION
8	5 or 6	Double	15 & Lower	Hit
9	3	Double	15 & Lower	Hit
10 or 11	2	Hit	Any count	Hit
10 or 11	3	Double	10 & Lower	Hit
10	8	Hit	57 & Higher	Double
10 or 11	9	Hit	64 & Higher	Double
11	8	Double	10 or Lower	Hit
12	4-5-6	Stand	10 or Lower	Hit
13	2-3	Stand	10 or Lower	Hit
13	4-5-6	Stand	7 or Lower	Hit
14	2-3	Stand	7 or Lower	Hit
14	7 thru Ace	Hit	52 or Higher	Stand
15	7 thru Ace	Hit	49 or Higher	Stand
16	7 thru Ace	Hit	49 or Higher	Stand
A-2	4	Hit	57 or Higher	Double
A-3,A-4,A-5	3	Hit	57 or Higher	Double
A-6	3	Double	15 or Lower	Hit
A-7	3	Double	15 or Lower	Stand
A-A	2	Hit	Any count	Hit
A-A	3	Split	10 or Lower	Hit
A-A	4	Split	7 or Lower	Hit
A-A	8	Split	10 or Lower	Hit
A-A	9	Hit	57 or Higher	Split

70

STANDING HAND

I intentionally left this chapter out, hoping you might question the use of my terminology: 'Standing hand of the dealer.'

Since the only card you see of the dealers is his up card, you don't have the opportunity of making your moves against his total hand, as the other card is face down.

There is only one thing hurting you in Blackjack:

1) Player does not get to see dealers buried card until after he makes his move, which a lot of times is too late.

That's it. That's the reason that Blackjack is the roughest game in the casino. The player has to make his decision first. So, you must be a strong player vs the only card you can see.

When the dealer shows a seven thru ace, it is called a standing hand cause he is in a position where all he has to do is expose his buried card and be in a standing position.

For instance, if he shows a queen, all he has to do is turn over a 7, 8, 9, 10, jack, queen, king, or ace to have 17 or better. That's 8 out of 13 times he doesn't have to hit. And since the only time anyone breaks is when he hits, this puts the dealer in the strong position of beating you — especially when some dope sits on a total of 12 through 16.

Even if the dealer turns over a 2-3-4-5 or 6 with that queen, his chances of catching a standing hand is an additional one in five, giving him 9 out of 13 chances of getting into a standing position, when he has ten thru ace as his up-card.

Suppose his up-card is a seven. A mere flick of the buried card could shoot up a 10, jack, queen, king or ace. The player sitting with a breaking hand is dead. Or, the dealer could turn over a 2, 3, 4, giving him a strong nine, ten or eleven to draw to.

That's why the term 'standing hand' should be completely understood. And when you have a breaking hand, you MUST hit it against the dealers standing card of 7 thru ace, when you are playing against a neutral shoe. The lack of understanding this position by the dealer is crushing the novice Blackjack player. You better not be in that group.

71

BREAKING HAND

Again, I've left this chapter out, using it to reinforce your Knowledge when you get to this point. It is similar to the explanation of the dealer being in a standing position, only this time he is in trouble.

When the dealers up-card is a 2, 3, 4, 5 or 6, he is said to be in a breaking position, because no matter what he turns over, he must hit. And that is the only way he'll break.

I know, I know, I know, you're dying to correct me on the six. G.I. Wettem just wet his pants, he got so excited wanting to correct me.

He wants me to know that if the dealer shows a six as his up card, there is a one in thirteen chance that he could turn over an ace and be in a position of having a soft seventeen and doesn't have to hit.

G.I. Wettem is right. Not for wetting his pants, but by bringing this situation up. There have been more controlled parties who also are aware of this, but still counted that six as the dealer being in a hole and calling it a breaking hand.

Before this poor guy next ruins his shoes, let me explain further. While it is true that this situation could come up, the odds are 12 in 13 against it happening and that percentage is in your favor. You must take that into consideration.

I'm aware he could turn over an ace and have a standing 17, but when he turns over a ten value card he's in a lot of trouble. In fact, he's worse off hitting the 16 than banging against a twelve or thirteen and that's why the

177

strong player likes to see the dealer showing a six.

So you with the soaking pants, standing in that pool of water — take a second look before you start making waves (a pun). When the dealer shows a six, he is in trouble. We consider it a breaking hand.

G.I. Wettem is right on one hand, but the overall outlook in that situation weighs in favor of calling that six a breaking hand and I'll bet he likes to see the dealer show that six, rather than a two or three.

I gotta close this chapter fast, there's a guy in an uncomfortable situation, dying to get into dry clothes.

72

YOU HAVE 8 THROUGH 11

Right at the top of the page on the Variation Chart, we see your hand of 8, 9, 10 or 11 vs the dealers breaking hand. My basic strategy tells you to double your eight vs the dealers 5 or 6, cause he's in trouble and you wanna whack him.

But when the count is 15 or lower, your chances of getting a small card has increased, so I want you to merely hit that 8.

Same is true for the nine vs the dealers 3. When the count reaches 15 or lower you should hit, not double.

Continue down to your 10 or 11 vs the dealers 2 or 3. You'll notice I have you hitting rather than doubling when the deck is poor. Make sure you zero in on this move and don't make the mistake of doubling 10 or 11 against the dealers strong neutral cards of 2 or 3.

The poorness of the count makes it highly probable you'll get a low card for your double down and the dealer will probably not break, as he is hitting his 2 or 3 with a poor deck. Don't deviate from this variation. You're putting yourself in the position of losing a double bet.

This rule also covers two fives vs the dealers 2 or 3. Hit those tens, don't double. These are important variables, so don't go nodding in agreement and then going out and doing the opposite.

73

10 OR 11 VS. 8 OR 9

You know what an advocate I am about the theory of hitting tens and elevens vs the dealers power cards.

I say the Rosary for every player I see doubling a ten against the dealers 9 or 10 or ace. It amazes me how this rule has been allowed to steamroll thru the years, with millions of players adhering to it's call.

I've said it 100,000 times. Hit — do not double the 10 or 11 vs the dealers nine thru ace. But, my wails fall mostly on deaf ears. It's a pity.

OK, you doubting Thomas' — here's where you have my blessings to double the 10 or 11 vs the 8 or 9. It's all right to double the 10 against the eight when count reaches 57 or higher, and to bang a double down bet on your 10 or 11 when dealer shows a nine and count is 64 or higher.

In these cases you've got a rich deck, giving you a good chance to pick up a 20 or 21 and whack his possible 18 or 19.

When the deck is neutral or only slightly rich, it is still a no-no to double that 10 or 11, but at least you get a few chances to do your dirty deed of doubling against the dealers stronger cards. That time is only when the running count is in a rich position.

74

COUNT IS 10 OR LOWER

We've already touched on these moves and they're so logical that is doesn't take much explaining to show why.

When you're in a breaking position of 12, 13, or 14 and the shoe is poor, like 10 or lower, you have a bevy of small cards waiting to slide out of that shoe.

The variation chart changes the basic rule of standing with these breaking hands, due to the fact you're not in a rotten position and even if you stayed with your low breaking hands, the dealer will probably catch a small card.

You've got a double edged sword here, so it behooves you to hit rather than stand.

This rule also applies when you have 14 vs the dealers 2 or 3. I know it's tough to hit that 14, but the extra edge of knowing the shoe is 'poor' lessens the blow. Here is where you can apply your own variables. I say hit the 14 against the dealers 2 and 3 when count reaches 7. Maybe you want to wait until it's 6 or 5. That's your choice. I give you the meat of the Theory, you start cooking with these moves when you feel ready.

If the count is poor (7) and the shoe shows only one deck remaining, get to banging that 14 vs the 2 or 3. If there are three decks left, you might like to see the count drop another notch or two.

With these moves, you'll break less times cause of the low running count and thereby can stay in the game longer.

Getting the drift???

75

TOUGH MOVES

On the variation chart it states that when you have a 14, 15, or 16 against the dealers standing hand, you must stand when the deck is rich. That's a tough pill for the strong player to swallow.

By now you realize the logic of this move, cause hitting those breaking hands is sure to bring disaster when that deck is rich in tens. Yet I still have people tell me that if they have a 15 and the dealer shows a queen and the deck is rich, he is sure to catch that picture and beat you anyhow.

A very logical assumption. And the people asking that question have all the right in the world to bring it up. The argument could go on for years, with neither side gaining a proper answer.

So it comes down to having to make a decision. I strongly advise you to 'stand' in these situations and go with the possibility that the dealer has a lousy four or five or some other breaking card hidden under his up card of queen. Now he must hit into the rich deck and take his licking.

It's a tough stand, but once you get the hang of counting, you'll feel very easy about making these moves. You'll even add some of your own.

Notice that I say stand with a 14 against the dealers standing hand, when count reaches 52. You might be at a table where there is only a half deck left in that shoe and the count is only 49. You will decide to stand, instead of waiting for the count to reach 52 and you'd be 100% correct.

There will be literally thousands of these moves and while a lot of them will be tough to do, the logical thing always turns out to be the best way — in the long run.

76

DOUBLING THE SOFT HANDS

These variations of basic strategy will be a little harder to comprehend, but as you go along, you'll see the benefit of making adjustments.

Start with the first soft change on the Variations Chart: ace/deuce vs the dealers 4. Basic strategy dictates a hit, but now you'll go for a double down when count reaches 57 and higher. There are two reasons:

1) deck is rich and dealer 'probably' has ten card buried,
2) in this case, he'll 'probably' catch a breaking card.

This is an instance where you must rely on the laws of probability being in your favor — due to the richness of the count.

Forget about what your double down card could be. It isn't even important. You want that dealer banging his breaking hand with a rich deck.

Sliding down to the next example on the chart, we see the soft 14, 15 and 16 vs the dealer's three. Basic strategy says hit.

Again the same reasoning applies and we double when count climbs to 57 and up. This becomes a super strong move when the shoe is down to its last one or two decks.

The higher the count, the more likely you are to pick up this double victory. Hope you're getting the grasp of this Theory.

In the matter of side count of aces, you can see how

important that exercise is now. Suppose you have a count of 59 and a plus 4 aces in that shoe.

Your chances of getting Blackjack is better and if you do happen to reach a soft double vs the dealers breaking hand, your chances of winning is vastly improved.

I know the richness of the deck indicates he may have a ten as his up card, but in the instances when he doesn't — you're sitting with a loaded gun to his gut.

77

SOFT HANDS VS. LOW COUNT

Now we slide to the soft hands when the count is poor.

A soft 17 (ace/six) calls for a double against the dealers three in basic strategy. When count drops to 15 and lower, change that to a hit.

The reason is the dealer is not that weak with the three and is not in a high percentage breaking position. This is a definite hit.

Same reasoning follows with your soft eighteen (ace/seven) against his three. With basic strategy, you would double on a neutral count. In this case, just stand with your 18 when count is down to 15 and lower. It's safer.

I don't wanna go into a multitude of examples on the variations of soft hands. It is your job to see that changes in basic play will come up as the count rises. Learn to make instant changes with these strong double down soft hands.

78

TWO ACES

I've been dying to get to these examples. My greatest satisfaction in teaching gambling is to hear a strong player tell me he has now swung over to my theory of handling aces and it has done wonders for him.

I am an avid believer in the art of utilizing the ace to the fullest against the house. In a previous chapter I mentioned that if you were given an ace in every hand you played, you could quit your $80,000 a year job and bang the casinos day after day.

Since that will never happen, let's go to the next level. When you do get an ace or — heavens to Betsy — two aces, be smart enough to make them count.

Now you know — or God help you — you should know, that I only split aces vs the dealers 3 thru 7.

Card counting determines my other splitting moves. And these are the instances I hope you will agree with me to the fullest.

I've already told you about two aces vs the deuce. I'd like you to hit all the time, regardless of the count.

Move down to two aces against the three or four. Usually that calls for a split, but as that count keeps dropping, your chances of getting small cards is increasing and the move is to hit, not split.

Logically, look at a plus factor with hitting two aces in a poor count. When that count is 10 and down, there's a good chance you could catch a five on one ace and a three on the other. Two rotten hands.

Also, the dealer is pulling to a poor count and doesn't have the deadly breaking tens to worry about.

Suppose you hit your two aces and pulled that five and three. Now you have one solid hand of 20, instead of two stinkers. Getting the point?

Next move is two aces vs the dealers 8. When count reaches 10 and lower, I don't even want you aggressive splitters of aces vs the 8 to continue to split.

The deck is too poor to give you a good pull. Hit those aces all the time in poor counts.

Now I bite my tongue on the next move, because the percentage is in my favor. With poor, neutral, or medium rich counts, the proper decision is to hit aces against the nine. But when the count is 57 and higher, you have a good chance of pulling tens, especially near the end of the shoe, so a variation pops up.

Split the aces against the nine. Man, how I detest saying that and yet it is a strong move and gets stronger as the count rises.

How about splitting aces vs the dealers ten or ace? NO!!!

How about if the count is 60? NO!!!

Well, how about if it's 70? NO!!! Positively, NO!!!

I'll let you split aces vs the dealers nine when count reaches 57 or higher, but that's it. Absolutely no splitting against the tens or aces.

That's it on the splitting of aces. In a nutshell, I want you to savor the power of those cards. They will bang out a lot of wins for you.

But learn the discipline of knowing how to handle them.

79

DOUBLING ACES

I don't wanna waste a lot of time explaining this silly move, but you'd be surprised how many people raise this question.

There is absolutely no logic in doubling aces. The reason you split and double down, is to get more money against that dealer when he's in trouble.

But I fail to see the edge for the player in doubling two aces — instead of going for a split. It is my humble opinion, that the people who bring up this example are just attempting to create a stir and make others think they've come up with some super move.

I don't believe any of those players actually put it into play, but it gives them the aura of making them sound like they know what they're saying, simply because it's an 'odd' move.

It ain't odd, it's stupid. How could anyone with an ounce of intelligence, even suggest doubling the amount of money they have at risk and then be in a position to lose that money, with no real edge going for them.

Never double aces against any card, regardless of the count, never, never, ever, ever, never, ever, never...

80

DOUBLING THE 12

We're about finished with the Knowledge section of this book, but I just wanna wind it down with some personal opinions. The next two chapters cover the most popular questions I get on Blackjack.

Now mind you, the people asking these questions don't realize that in the long run — the only thing that separates the winners from the losers is Money Management and Discipline.

But since these subjects are such thorns in their sides, it's best that we touch on them and at the same time, give you my humble opinion.

DOUBLING THE 12: Of all the nonsense. When this question comes up, I sneak a look around the room to see if there are any nodding heads, as if someone else also had that thought cross his mind.

Sure enough, there's always another two or three with the same thought, bobbing their heads up and down. So I bite my tongue, take a deep breath and promise to explain it in a calm matter: ''Anybody who even thinks of doubling a twelve, regardless of the count, is a first class jerk.'' And from there I get nasty — or is the work nastier?

The Theory of doubling down and splitting, is to get more money against the dealers weak card and I just went over this in chapter 77.

The questioner always comes back and says he doubles only when the dealer has a 4-5-6 and only when the count is poor.

But you must look at the other side of the coin. There is not one single double down or split move in basic strategy, that calls for one of these moves, when you are in trouble of breaking and there-in lies the fallacy of this situation.

Even if the count is zero or lower, there is still the remote chance that a 10, jack, queen or king could appear and bust that hand of 12.

As long as even the slightest possibility of losing twice as much of your initial bet exists, don't do it. What's to be gained? The deck is poor, you'll probably get a low card and he'll probably get a low hit on his 4-5-6. Since he isn't in a terribly bad breaking position, you're giving him too much room to out draw you.

Does that make sense to you? Well it should, cause it gives a logical explanation as to why you should never double a 12 against any card — regardless of the running count.

It's a move that is stupid, period.

81

SHOULD I PLAY TWO HANDS?

When you get to the Money Management section, you'll see how the Bankroll chapters mesh into the handling of your money.

Actually, you don't have the right to decide if you should play two hands or not, as your starting Bankroll is the sole judge of how much you bet.

You'll be getting an earful of that pretty soon, but I can almost hear the questions from you aggressive players..."Yeah, but what if the deck is rich? Shouldn't I take advantage of it?"

It was only a few chapters back that I answered this question — before it was put forth. Or how many of you have already forgotten?

I do not believe that the richness of the deck gives you the right to bet extra amounts of money — just like I don't believe the theory of increasing your bets to crazy levels is such a good idea, just because of that high count. Betting two hands falls into that classification.

I play Blackjack cause I can count cards. There are many times I back-count, find a very rich or very poor shoe and immediately jump into that game.

On some occasions I will play two hands. That's because I have the proper Bankroll to go along with an awareness of that accurate count.

The fact I have the Bankroll gives me the right to bet two or three or four hands at a time, or even the whole darn table. Bottom line is I have the Bankroll, Knowledge of the Game, Money Management and Discipline. The same goes for you. If you don't got the bread to play multiple hands, then you shouldn't do it. In fact, if you don't have all facets of the Big 4 you shouldn't even think about playing one hand. Only a dope would risk his money in a game where he ain't perfect.

Several months ago I was in Harrah's Marina in Atlantic City, taking my daughters, Lori and Colleen, to see a show. After the show we had dinner and the girls wanted to go up to the room, watch a little TV, and go to bed.

Since they are too young to go into the casinos, I had an idea what they were doing — giving me the opportunity to play a little. I only had a couple of hundred dollars on me, so a five dollar table was my target. It took me over an hour to chart and backcount a game, with an opening at first base.

Finally I caught a table where the first three hands shot out non-tens like a machine gun. The count shot right up to fifty five and showed a plus four in aces. I bought in for two hundred and won the first six hands. The count climbed into the low sixties and maintained a plus on the aces. I absolutely refused to bet two hands, until my profit reached two hundred dollars. Then I put half in my pocket and started to play two hands, but only after my profit was safely tucked away.

I knew when I sat down that the deck was rich, but my Bankroll controls the amount of hands and the amount of the bets. When the shoe ended, I went back to one hand, played a little longer and left the table a few hundred dollars to the good. That is the type of control I want you to exhibit.

82

TEAMS

Now we're getting a little advanced. This is the art of two or more people working together in a casino.

A lot of teams even employ six and eight people to perfect their plan. Here's how it works. Each of these people are expert counters. They enter a casino separately and begin to cover their previously designated tables.

They fan out, with each partner having about six or eight tables to chart. They are back-counting when a shoe comes out — looking only for that shoe to reach a 'rich' count.

Since there are different methods of counting and different numbers that key the richness of a shoe, I sure as heck ain't gonna go over every system in the world. Just understand that they wait for their 'rich' point.

Suppose we had a team of eight players using my system. Each member is looking for the count to reach 49, which indicates it is rich and signals for another member to go to the table.

Since every shoe does not bring out a 'rich' or 'poor' designation during the course of a series of hands, it's fairly obvious that you may go two hours before finding a table that has a 'rich' count.

The thing is that you wanna be in on the game when it does happen. If you're working alone, you're restricted as to how many tables you can chart at once.

A six and eight team of men and women can cover more tables, increasing their chances of getting the hot shoe, or at least the 'rich' shoe.

When you perfect this counting method and head for the casinos, you'll be working alone and must take pot-shots at each table, standing and watching, sometimes for hours, before that game shoots out a 'rich' count.

That's if you have decided to play only at tables where the count reaches the rich point. To do that, you must stand and count at the tables you choose to watch. A counting team can move all over a casino, picking their spots.

Sometimes a whole day goes by without these partners even exchanging one word. They enter the casino at staggered times and go to their appointed section. They'll go to a game where the shoe is just coming out, start their count and wait for a heavy swing in the running count.

The rules of their team play are carefully laid out and no teams work the same way. They may have theories that they pre-set and follow to a T.

Here's some examples a counter may be looking for:
1) Stay at a table until he counts only 3 shoes,
2) Stay at a table and count only the first half of that shoe and then move to the next table,
3) Look only for the count to reach 49,
4) Look for the count to reach high neutral (maybe 40),
5) Wait until shoe is fairly deep, coinciding with a rich count of 55,
6) Wait until count reaches 55, regardless of decks remaining,
7) Utilize count of 15 and lower,
8) Have a prescribed number that counter will reach, before making signal to other partners.

These examples are a few that teams use and the person standing behind the table keeping the count has the job of merely counting. He will NOT play at that table.

Let's suppose this particular team has set 45 as it's key. The assigned partner at that table is not playing, but standing and back counting. The count reaches the 'medium rich' point of 40, heading towards the key that was set.

He gives a signal...which we'll go over a few chapters from now. The signal is picked up by a roving partner, who is waiting for the indication that a shoe is in 'medium rich' position and he heads for that table. Chapter 82 picks up the rovers next step.

This gives you an idea of why players work in teams. They cover a lot of tables and are bound to find rich shoes.

Remember what I said about the ability of these partners. Every one of them is a dynamite counter. There is no room for error.

83

SPOTTING A COUNTER

You know, the pit bosses and floor people in a casino were not born two weeks ago. They are aware of the power of card counting and are very proficient in picking out counters at a table.

One of the reasons it's so easy to spot a counter is because there are so many dopes in the games, that a good player stands out.

Personally, I can stand at a table and spot the very good players in a matter of five or six hands. Since there are so few counters, and I mean bonafide experts, the bad player brings attention to himself by his lack of the proper use of basic strategy.

It's rough to go the next step and find the counter, cause they only surface when the deck becomes 'rich.' The rest of the time they'll only show as strong basic players.

A spotter for the casino would have to know when a deck is rich, to be able to zero in on the true pro. But after a while they notice patterns that key them to a strong player.

In Atlantic City, card counters are not penalized. They are not banished from the casino as they were years ago. The courts have ruled that counting is not illegal.

However, the house has the right to call for a shuffle anytime they wish and this will neutralize the counter.

Suppose Surely Sharp is sitting at a table, patiently counting through six shoes and finally catches a scorching hot game. She adjusts both her strategy and her bets. Now she sits back and waits for a segment of rich cards to pour out of the shoe.

Along comes a very sharp floor person and orders the dealer to reshuffle the deck, breaking Surely's heart.

They can do this any time they like. It will irritate the other players, but it is the counter that the house is trying to foil...and do.

That's why teams working a casino must be very discreet, in order to avoid being detected. Of course there's the other side of the coin, where a blackjack player just loves to be pointed out as a counter.

Blabb L. Tounge is a blackjack player who thinks he is very good. He also thinks he is a counter, cause when he sees six small cards in the previous few hands show up, he immediately assumes the deck is rich and the tens will come spilling out. He bets $100 on the next hand, loses, and goes to $200 and loses again. He drops $400 on the table and gets whacked.

He's at the table limit and wants to bet $800. He asks the floor person for an OK to raise his bet to $800. The floor person hesitates in his decision. Old Blabb L. Tounge spits out his nonsense: "Hey man, the deck is rich, I wanna cash in on it."

Right away the floor person smells counter and declines the request. The Blabb bets $500 and again loses. This time the floor person instructs the dealer to reshuffle, bringing the deck back to neutral. He doesn't realize that the stooge with the mouth is not really a counter.

Our hero, out a quick $1200, gives a smirk and slides off the stool. He walks away grumbling out loud that legitimate counters are being taken advantage of. But secretly he was happy that the floor person took him for a counter. Of all the crock...instead of bemoaning the loss of the money, he rushes to tell his friends that he was 'discovered' as being a counter.

They have stalls in stables for jack-asses like that. But an idiot like this would take it as a step up in life. They just love the thrill of being noticed in a casino. But the powers that be in a casino recognize these jerks and give them a lot of ground, figuring they'll hang themselves. The jerks bring their own ropes.

Let's say a team partner is scheduled to back count six tables in section (a) from 11 am to noon. Then he will switch over to a set of tables in section (d). This way he doesn't spend a lot of time in a particular section and stand the chance of being noticed.

Also, there are things that the back counter must do to try and divert attention from himself. Following are some of the things a team partner may do to try and conceal being noticed:

- a) dress sloppily,
- b) don't stay at one table too long,
- c) look bored,
- d) act disinterested,
  - 1) maybe he's back counting a table and it comes toward the end of a shoe and he knows he won't reach a rich point. He'll leave that section and get a drink of water or look over a roulette game or crap table, then saunder back to his station.
- e) act like he's just hanging around, waiting for his wife, by constantly looking at his watch and indicating disgust.

These team players are experts in diverting attention from themselves, much unlike our hero, Blabb L. Tounge.

Once the floor person decides you ain't worth watching, you're able to cruise around your section at will.

Remember, the six or eight tables a partner is assigned to may not necessarily be in the same section. They may have four tables in section (b) and four in section (f). Pretty tough to nail that guy as a counter.

Team play is an art. You ain't taking on dopes when you enter a casino!

84

THE SIGNAL

Once a back counter has reached the appointed number he is seeking, it is his job to get another partner to that table, to begin play.

Usually a team player will not sit at the table he is counting behind, as the floor people will soon pick up the fact that he only plays at tables where he has spent considerable time watching the game. Eventually they'll read him as a counter.

Also, he never plays at the beginning of a shoe, which means he's never involved in a neutral game. It doesn't take these floor people long to zero in.

So the team counter will signal a partner to come to the table he is back counting, when it reaches the pre-set number. Let's say 43 was the point at which the counter signals someone to come to that table.

He will have a bevy of moves that a partner in another section is waiting to receive. This partner could be two aisles over, but he is watching the back-counter, waiting for a signal.

The count hits 43 and the signal goes out. It could be any one of the following:

1) Scratch the right ear,
2) Hold your watch to your left ear to see if it's ticking,
3) Put a pencil in your ear,
4) Take off your jacket,
5) Or put on your jacket,

6) Loosen your tie,

7) Take off your tie,

8) Merely open the top button of your shirt,

9) Kiss the cocktail waitress as she goes by.

Number nine has nothing to do with signalling a partner to the table. It's just a signal that this back-counter is getting a little excited, watching the cocktail waitress parade by and he just felt like giving her a little peck.

There are literally dozens of signals that the counter will give, that alerts the person who will become the player.

Suppose the counter flashes the predetermined sign to the player that the count is at 43 (that might be #5 above).

The player immediately heads for that table, but acting like he's just strolling along, looking for a spot to play.

When he received his signal, the appointed number was 43, and he moves to that table. When he gets there, the counter brings him up to date with the count.

He may scratch the right side of his face with his right hand. Each part of his body is a number, keyed off the right hand:

a) Neck 43

b) Nose 44

c) Ear 45

d) Cheek 46

e) Head 47

f) Eye 48

g) Mouth 49

h) Throat 50

i) Shoulder 51

j) Chest 52

k) Stomach . . . . counter is hungry

If the move is made with the left hand, it may indicate count has dropped beneath key of 43. So, the counter signals the player with his left hand.

- a) Chest 42
- b) Shoulder 41
- c) Throat 40
- d) Mouth 39
- e) Eye 38
- f) Head 37

And so on...you get the drift.

The cut-of is the end of the hand. When the ongoing hand is over, the counter gives his final count and the player acknowledges by maybe taking off his jacket. The player buys in and gets ready to play.

The back-counter stays around for a few hands and then walks off, looking to pick up his duties at another table.

Back to the player. If he got in on a rich count, he begins his play at an opportune time. If the count is a click or two away, he will wait for that hand to be finished, but in the meantime picks up the count.

He may wait for the deck to reach 50 or 52 or 54 or whatever, and play at the table only while the count is in the mid-fifties and up.

A slick counting move has been accomplished and the counter has adroitly brought in the player, without anyone noticing.

The player will stay at the table until the shoe ends or the count drops back to neutral. But he is always involved in a 'rich' count.

When he leaves that game, he'll return to his station and await one of the counters giving him a signal to go to another table.

85

SIX DECK DESIGNATION

I probably gave you this in bits and pieces before, but now it's time to put it all together into chart form.

It is the designation of the running count, based on the play at a six deck shoe. Ain't gonna hurt you to memorize this chart and the one in the next chapter. It'll keep you keyed onto the variations you must make at different points of your running count:

a)	Neutral	20 to 30
b)	Medium Neutral	31 to 40
c)	Strong Neutral	41 to 48
d)	Medium Poor	19 to 15
e)	Poor	14 to 8
f)	Very poor	7 to 2
g)	Very, very poor	1 and negative 0
h)	Rich	49 to 56
i)	Very rich	57 to 63
j)	Very, very rich	64 and up

Very simple to grasp what the chart does for you. It sets the different stages of your 'running count' into classifications of poor, neutral and rich.

With the variation chart, you will make the moves called for, due to the imbalance in the shoe, and this chart shows you how to classify the shoe as it hits the different numbers.

The Money Management sections will show you systems on how to apply your bet, according to the 'running count.' This is simply to make you aware of where the changes take place as the game flows. Don't worry, you'll soon put these figures to full memory and it'll easily become a part of your game.

The two charts I am giving you are for six and eight deck games, which will be similar to the four deck game, where-in you can make the simple adjustment in the neutral phase. Same is true when you find a two deck game. Use a spin-off from the one deck chart. I want you to be able to work this out.

86

EIGHT DECK DESIGNATION

Same story as previous chapter, only this is based on an 8 deck game. I'm giving you the designations for both starting at 17 and getting rich at 49, and starting at 27, using 59 as the rich point.

Count starting at 17:

a) Neutral . . . . 13 to 30
b) Medium Neutral . . . . 31 to 40
c) Strong Neutral . . . . 41 to 48
d) Medium poor . . . . 12 to 8
e) Poor . . . . 7 to 2
f) Very poor . . . . 1 and negative 0
g) Rich . . . . 49 to 56
h) Very rich . . . . 57 to 63
i) Very, very rich . . . . 64 and up

Pretty similar to 6 decks, except classification of very poor and very, very poor is linked together when it gets down to negative 0. At that point you've got a deck pretty well devoid of tens.

Count starting at 27 and getting rich at 59:

a) Neutral . . . . 20 to 35
b) Medium neutral . . . . 36 to 46
c) Strong Neutral . . . . 47 to 58
d) Medium poor . . . . 19 to 14
e) Poor . . . . 13 to 7
f) Very poor . . . . 6 to 0
g) Very, very poor . . . . Negative 0

   h) Rich . . . . .59 to 66

   i) Very rich . . . . .67 to 74

   j) Very, very rich . . . . .75 and up

I think you get the point and you'll be surprised how quickly you pick this up.

But please, please spend a few minutes to absorb the next message.

The **LESS** decks there are to play in the shoe, the more powerful the 'running count' and the stronger the designation of the shape of that shoe will become. This point is so important and yet so simple, I don't wanna miss even one of you from grasping it's impact.

One more time: A 'rich' count of 57 for example, is tons of times more important when there is only one deck left to come out, then the same count with three decks still left to be dealt.

Keep your eyes glued to that discard tray. For instance, if you have to choose between watching that discard tray and catching a quick glimpse of the cocktail waitress wiggling down the aisle, you know what you **should** do. Watch that tray.

I know what **I'd** do...but that's another story. Just watch the tray.

Bottom line is that you catch the point during that game where you have it all going for you:

   1) Rich count,

   2) One deck remaining,

   3) Dealer in cold run, turning over weak cards,

   4) Cocktail waitress approaching table while dealer is shuffling and you don't have to watch the tray.

When all those things are happening, you'll see the power of learning how to count.

87

WRAPPING UP KNOWLEDGE

Thank God!! Dozens of chapters on Knowledge of the Game. I never thought the end would come. I tried to keep the chapters short, so as to let the message of each part of counting sink in and yet not become boring.

I'm not gonna review every part of counting, as it'd be too redundant. If you wanna check on a certain matter, just slip back to that particular chapter and go over it.

But there are several points I wanna drive home. Some of these things you should remember, just by the reminder. The ones you have questions about, spend some time and perfect their message:

a) Have your count down to 12-13 seconds per deck,

b) Be perfect in Basic Strategy,

c) Have card recognition perfected,

d) Memorize the Variation chart,

e) Be sure you know when shoe is approaching different stages, such as 'poor,' 'neutral,' or 'rich,'

f) Make sure you know the variations to apply to basic strategy, based on 'running count' and remaining decks,

g) Know how to recognize 'pure richness' of a shoe, based on those remaining decks,

h) Keep constant check on discard tray,

i) Know how to back-count at a table before joining the game,

1) Back-counting is strictly optional. If you put a gun to my head, I'd say back-count, but you decide.

j) Chart the table by checking out dealers up card (important),

k) Use both the charting of the table, along with back-counting to determine if you will play at that game,

l) Decide at what point in the 'running count' you will join the game (40 or 43 or 47 or 49, etc.).

NOTE: Some of you will back-count a table before playing and join the game at a count that you will predetermine. Others will sit at a table and start their play when the shoe first comes out. This is strictly up to each individual to make up his or her mind. It takes a lot more patience and Discipline to chart and back-count. While it is a grinding process, it is more effective.

In a nutshell, this covers the second part of the Big 4: Knowledge of the Game. All I've done in this section is cover the way to count. I've given you my Theory...to use card counting to improve your basic strategy. I heartily believe that this is the way to perfect your attack on the game of Blackjack.

Don't forget — I've only shown you how to count and how to use the Knowledge of the count. I haven't even gotten into how to bet and when to walk — the meat of gambling.

Do not turn the page to the next section until you are perfect in the complete understanding of the Theory of card counting and have your speed at a constant 12-13 seconds per deck.

MONEY MANAGEMENT 88

WHAT IS MONEY MANAGEMENT?

There's a popular saying that goes something like this: "Everybody talks about the weather, but nobody does anything about it."

The same is said for 95% of the people who gamble: "Everybody knows they need Money Management, but they don't do a blessed thing about getting it.

I'll explain what it is and how it will absolutely revolutionize your gambling forays. The fact that I'll show you what it is will not do that changing...that part is up to you. If you don't have the intelligence to practice Money Management, that's your problem. So it behooves you to absorb this entire section.

This is the third part of the Big 4 and the motor that keeps you running toward a successful day. Take this advice with an open mind. The Theory is based on a conservative approach, but give it a pop.

All the Knowledge in the world ain't gonna do diddedly dang for you if you don't know how to bet. The lack of manipulating your chips will eventually cause your downfall.

You already know that the "Bankroll" is the part of the Big 4 that makes every monetary decision for you, such as:

1) Sets Win Goal for each Session and for your day,

2) Sets Loss Limit for each Session and for your day,

3)   Determines the amount you take to each Session,

4)   Sets the pattern for your Series bets.

"Money Management" takes that Bankroll and controls each and every bet of a Series. Since the Bankroll already determined the Win Goal and Loss Limit of a Session, the Money Management you practice, helps put you in the direction of reaching that Win Goal.

Money Management will tell you every bet to make after a win and every bet to make after a loss. In other words, the Series bets will be determined beforehand and not a decision that is made by your feelings or whims.

In effect, you are really a robot and programmed to make bets that you set, before you even reached the table.

Iva Feelin has absolutely no idea what his bet will be after a winning or losing hand. He operates strictly on how he feels when the dealer prepares to come out with the next hand. He has a batch of chips in his palm and places them on the lay-out, in a short or high stack, depending on this feeling. His silly options depend on this thinking:

a)   I lost the last hand, so I'm due to win,

b)   I won the last hand, so I'm due to lose,

c)   The dealer looks tired, he'll probably break,

d)   The cocktail waitress gave me a sly smile, it should bring me luck, so I'll increase my bet,

e)   I've won 8 hands in a row and the pit boss is looking at me in an odd way. I'll bet small so he doesn't get mad,

f)   I've got an itchy scalp. That usually means something good will happen, so I'll bet $100 (it probably means he has dandruff).

You think these are silly statements? I have a strong feeling about the Iva Feelins of the gambling world. I feel they're nuts. Anyone who makes wagers, based on feelings or hunches or assumptions has a problem. I don't think he's dealing with a full deck.

You want a good laugh? Walk up and down a group of Blackjack tables in the casinos and watch the ill-planned, nonsensical betting patterns of the patrons.

Most of their wagers are based strictly on how they 'think' they will do on the up-coming hand. There is no pattern to their bets. Lettar Ide bets $10, wins and lets the whole $20 ride on the next hand. Again he wins, has $40, and again he lets it all ride. Bang, he wins again, has $80, and screams loud enough for the people eight tables down to hear: "Let 'er ride," and shoves the whole $80 into play.

This time he loses and you'd think the world ended. He starts screaming about his rotten luck, not even realizing he won three out of four hands and is out $10. Now that's a rotten player. Lettar Ide has no Money Management.

Go ahead, check out those tables — watch the silly pattern of illogical bets. The faces change, the stupidity stays on.

What is Money Management? It is a strict, disciplined, predetermined plan, that controls every single bet you make during the course of a day. **Every single bet**...whether it be a win or a loss.

If you don't got Money Management, you ain't got a prayer of a chance of winning consistently.

That may be lousy English, but it sure is good advice.

89

REGRESSION SYSTEM

If you read my books on Blackjack, Roulette or Baccarat, you know exactly what this system is about. Each of those books contain this extremely powerful method of play.

If you think you have perfected this method, go to sleep for the next few chapters. But if you're not perfect in your grasp of the Regression system and it's variations, then absorb this information again.

Gambling has been around since Eve uttered the infamous words to Adam: "I'll 'bet' you ain't got the guts to eat that apple!"

Naturally, the jerk bit — in more ways than one.

People have been gambling ever since. And usually losing. That's because the 'Theory' of wagering that has been copied and handed down thru the years, generation upon generation, is a rotten lousy one.

My 'Theory' is of a conservative nature, based upon the fact that we are taking on a game that offers us only a 50-50 chance of winning, minus the added vig that is attached to each game.

Just dwell on the fact that we never have more than a 50-50 chance of winning any bet we make. For that reason, I came up with a method of betting that has kept me solvent for many years.

The method is called the Regression System and the idea is to reduce your bet after a win — rather than increase it, or keep it the same.

The reasoning is that you can win as many hands as the house and still show a profit.

The key is in the first bet after a win. You regress your bet down, thus locking up a profit. This is completely different than what you presently do.

Suppose you were playing in Las Vegas at a $1 minimum table. Your first bet would be $2. If you won that $2, you'd do the following:

    a) take back the $2 you originally bet,

    b) take back one dollar of the $2 you won,

    c) your bet on that second hand would be $1.

It's as simple as A-B-C. Even if you lost that second bet, you would have back the $2 you started with, plus a $1 profit, cause you also took back one half of what you won on that first bet.

In essence, you won a bet and lost a bet, played the house even and still ended with a $1 profit.

That 'Series' was a stand-off with each side winning a hand, but you ended up on the plus side.

Get the drift?

90

OPPONENTS OF REGRESSION

Let's look at the other options that are open to you, after a winning bet. We'll still use $2 as the amount of your first wager. Suppose you win $2. This is what 99% of the people do:

1) Take back $2 and again bet $2,
2) Bet the whole $4,
3) Bet the whole $4 and even add a couple more chips.

These examples are the popular play of most people, so we'll set a table and have three contestants in action, with each one of these methods. Since gambling is a 50-50 proposition, we'll say each one lost the hand after their initial victory. Each used one of these methods, so let us analyze their approaches. Start with (#1).

This guy won a bet, lost a bet and is even with the house. He has to win the next bet or 67% of his hands to show a profit. With the Regression system you need win only 50%.

The guy with Theory (#2) is just too aggressive. If he loses that second bet, look at the position he is in. He won a bet, lost a bet, but ends up losing $2.

In other words, he won just as many hands as the house and ends up being out money. He ain't gonna last long with that type of thinking or betting. He is losing even when he plays the house to a stand-off. If he ever catches a hot dealer, he won't last long enough to even warm his seat.

Finally we get to player (#3) and his super aggressive mode of play. The bet he is making — where he adds chips to the original bet, plus the winning chips, is called a Paroli.

There is a time to bet a Paroli and that could be done in the middle of a scorching streak of wins during a 'Series.'

At that time you can take advantage of your hot run and take a deeper whack at the house. By that time you will have locked up a profit for that Series and a losing Paroli bet won't hurt you.

But making this type of bet after the first win is a foolish play. I think player (#2) is a jerk for betting his whole profit on the second hand.

You can imagine what I think of player (#3) for even thinking of adding more chips to that second bet. A loss will hurt him even worse than it will to (#2).

It's like the boob who get his thrills jumping off 2 story roof tops. Soon he wants bigger thrills and starts taking on bigger buildings. Pretty soon it's the 4 story building that gives him the biggest thrills. It's only a matter of time before the roof jumper and the bet jumper will both crash. One will run out of chips to bet, the other out of bones.

Opponents of the Regression will say that it is too timid and they wanna take advantage of a hot run right away.

Well, how do they know it's gonna be a hot run? The Regression system merely gives up the first win, to lock up a profit, and then you can get into your aggressive play.

The guy constantly looking for the gigantic returns will never move over to my Regression method. But if I can just convert a few people to the joy of winning consistent small amounts, my purpose with Money Management will have been fulfilled.

You don't like the Regression? I think you're making a mistake — a big one.

91

THEORY OF REGRESSION

You know by now that the 'theory' of the Regression is based on the fact that you can win a hand, lose a hand and end up with a profit.

For that reason the first bet of a series is always higher than the table minimum. This way you can regress back down to that minimum, with the difference being your profit.

Suppose you're at a $3 table. The first bet of your series would be $4 - $5 - $6 - $7 or $8, etc. After a win, you'd go back to $3.

We'll get into increasing series starting bets later on. Let's look at the negative possibilities first.

When you begin play at a Session, the amount of your buy-in will determine your betting Series. You should have 30 times the amount of that table minimum.

Suppose $150 is your buy-in and you're at a $5 table. You could make your first bet: $6 - $7 - $8 - $9 - $10 - etc.

Your first bet of the series is $8 for example. If you win, go down to $5 and now you're into a winning 'Series.' We'll go over the subsequent bets in the next chapter, don't get itchy.

If you lose that $5, the next Series will again begin with an eight dollar bet. You always revert back to the original bet, whenever the 'Series' ends.

However, we've got to be sure that after charting a table and making our buy-in, we don't run into a table that has turned completely cold. This betting method protects our money.

If you lose the first four hands of any Session, you immediately pick up and leave that table. That's a strict rule.

It is not mandatory that you stay at the same starting Series amount. Your first Series starts with $8. If you lose, the next series starts with $8. If you lose again, the third Series would begin at $7.

That's because this Session is taking on the appearance of a losing trend. If I'm in a losing trend, then I want my losses to be as small as possible.

Suppose we lose that third series bet which was $7, again on the first hand. My fourth 'Series' begins with $6.

If you lose that fourth series without a win showing, that horrible Session is over. You lost $8, $8, $7 and $6. The balance of your Session money is put in your pocket and you head off to chart another table, to begin another Session.

Notice that I kept reducing the starting amount, as the trend stayed against me. I did NOT start increasing my 'series' bets, with the illogical assumption that I was due to win. My losses at that Session were $29. Not a devastating amount at an ice cold table.

I'm content to bet small until that trend comes. It'll come.

92

UP AND PULL

Before sliding into this chapter, I beg you to have a clear head with your memory valves pumping in complete unison. This will show you how to use the Regression system. The variations are unlimited, so it is imperative that you grasp the theory of it and can apply your own off-shoots. This is an important part of your play and I call it 'Up and Pull.'

With the basic approach to the Regression System and using chips as increments of units, you play at a $5 table and start a Series at $10.

After a win, you'd go down to $5, then up to $10, then $15, then $20 and $25 and so on. All of this based on the fact that you kept winning during that Series.

If you played the above Series out on your living room rug, using buttons or pennies as chips, you'd see how this betting pattern would go.

As you got into the flow of a winning series, you'd be constantly increasing your bet and still pulling back a profit. Hence the term: 'Up and Pull.' Go thru a series:

- a) First bet $10...you win and regress down to $5,
- b) Second bet $5...you win and let the whole bet ride,
  - 1) The Series is already safe, with a $5 profit off the first win,
- c) Third bet $10...you win. Now you revert to

'Up and Pull.' Increase your next bet to $15 and pull back a $5 profit,

   1) At this point you have 'upped' your bet and 'pulled' back a profit,

  d) Fourth bet $15...you win. Option time has arrived for fifth bet:

    1) Same bet ($15) and you pull back profit of $15,

    2) Increase bet to $20 and pull back profit of $10,

    3) Increase bet to $25 and pull back profit of $5,

    4) Regress bet to $10 and pull back profit of $20,

    5) Regress bet to $5 and pull back profit of $25.

None of the above decisions are wrong, and the next chapter takes a look at the aggressive player vs the conservative one. Assume we continue the pattern of 'Up and Pull,' option (2). Our fifth bet would be $20, as we took back a profit of $10 and raised our Series bet from $15 to $20.

  e) Fifth bet $20...you win. Increase your wager to $25 and pull back profit of $15. At this point, wherein you won your bet of $20, you could have reverted to your own set of options as described under (d). Once you get into a winning Series, options will arrive at every level, after every winning hand (we're staying with simple increases now),

  f) Sixth bet $25...you lose. Series is over and next Series begins with bet of $10 and will follow the same pattern of the previous Series.

For the just completed Series you showed a profit of $35 and you were never in danger of getting hurt in that Series. Make sure you grasp the reasoning behind the Up and Pull' method.

When you get in a hot streak, you wanna bang out higher bets and make better returns. But since you never know when that streak will end, it's logical to keep stockpiling some profit, so that a winning Series doesn't turn into a frustrating, fruitless run.

Now don't tell me you got all of that with one reading. I can just picture that dork, Knod N. Agree, nodding his head up and down like he got the whole message in one glance down these pages.

'Up and Pull' is the method of my Money Management. I don't give a bird's butt what sequence of bets you use. That's none of my business. Once you lock up a profit after the first win, by regressing, your second bet to an amount less than the first one, you're in clover. How you increase your Series bets is your own decision...but pre-set those decisions and do NOT deviate. These are words of wisdom, O Ye of Little Faith. Heed them!!!

93

CONSERVATIVE VS. AGGRESSIVE

It doesn't make a hill of beans what a player sets up as his Regression Series, as long as he sticks to the basic concept of 'wanting to win.'

In the upper right hand corner of the cover of this book and every book I've written, are the four works that should be on every gamblers mind: "Learn How to Win."

Hey baby, that's an art, not something that you turn off and on like a light. You've gotta wanna win and you've gotta get in the habit of it.

Taake A. Chott drives to Atlantic City three times a month. All the way down in the car he makes silent prayers to God, begging for a winning day. He promises to say the Rosary every day for 6 months if he could just win $100.

Taake A. takes about 30 seconds finding a table. For two hours he bets very conservatively. All of a sudden he hits a nice streak and runs his profits up to $170. He is no longer interested in playing safe and conservative.

"Hey man, I'm down here for a good time, I'm up on the casino and it's time for me to take a good shot."

So Taake A. Chott takes his shot, with a strong aggressive betting pattern. I won't bore you with the blow-by-blow accounts of this poor dopes descent to the canvas, but the tide turns and the house sends him reeling on his back.

You've probably heard this story before and lived it a

few times yourself. Bottom line is that after Taake A. Chott did take his shot, he slinked back to his car...broke. Where were all his promises? He just got caught up in the aura of the game and completely lost control.

Set which way you want to bet, based on your Bankroll, and let that money decide your Win Goal. Don't deviate one dollar until that goal is reached. A chapter on 'Guarantees' and 'Excesses' explain how to handle that goal. If Taake A. Chott had taken a second to read that chapter, he'd have at least escaped with a profit when his trend turned.

If you start losing, stop playing and walk away. That ain't so hard to understand.

Go back to the previous chapter and look at how that winning series was handled with the 'Up and Pull' approach. The bets read: $10, $5, $10, $15, $20, $25. That's a very basic pattern.

Since I play conservative, I'd like to place a repeat wager somewhere along the line, in order to increase my profit potential for that Series.

When you reach the $15 level, make your next bet again $15 and pull back the $15 profit. This solidifies that Series as a profit maker. Now your series will read: $10, $5, $10, $15, $15, $20, $25.

You can also repeat again in that Series, at any level bet. This will all be spelled out in the chapter on Variations.

Go back again to the 4th bet of that Series, where it called for a $15 bet and you won. You could have become more aggressive and bet $25, pulling back a $5 profit. You wanna play aggressive — that's your choice.

Another thought for you conservative players. Still zeroing in on that $15 bet, you could make this move. Instead of raising your fifth bet to $20 or $25, you could have come up with a second Regression bet for that Series and made that fifth bet $10. That means you would bring $20 back to your pile.

The Series would then read: $10, $5, $10, $15, $10, $15, $20, $25.

Maybe you would use the super conservative approach, by making that fifth bet $5. Again you're putting two Regression moves in the same Series, and it would go: $10, $5, $10, $15, $5, $10, $15, $20, etc.

Your fifth bet was $5 and if you lose, you still show a nice profit of $35. That Series is over, and the next one begins with a bet of $10.

If aggressive is your style — go for it. If conservative is your choice, so be it. Whichever theory you operate under, stick to it. But don't jump back and forth with each successive Series. Use control.

94

OFF AMOUNTS

Oh how the casinos hate this bet, especially in Atlantic City. As we get deeper into this chapter, you'll see why I want you to bet 'off' amounts. But first you have to understand what it means in the first place.

Atlantic City is notorious for their high minimum bets and that has already been explained. Slowly they are going after the everyday player and putting in several $3 and $2 tables and that is tremendous. This allows the person with the short Bankroll to last longer, waiting for his trend.

By using the Regression method, you would bet $10, $5, $10, $15, $20, etc. Whether you want to admit it or not, this requirement of betting $10 on a hand of Blackjack, causes even the bravest of the brave to sweat a little. I'm talking to the majority of people who enter a casino, not the high roller.

Rightfully so that the majority of people sweat out a $10 wager. To many people, that's a heavy bet. They are just not financially or emotionally equipped with either the money or the guts to bet $10 a pop.

So when you buy in at a Session, I want you to immediately drop a couple of five dollar chips on the table and ask the dealer to 'break them down,' or 'give me some whites.'

You're asking him to give you dollar chips. This will allow you to start your Series at less than $10, but still be higher than the minimum.

Each series would begin with a bet of either $9, $8, $7 or $6. After a win, you'd regress down to $5 and now the variations of series bets has really increased.

With the 2-1-2 ($10-$5-$10) sequence, you can only increase or decrease in units of $5. Not so with the use of dollar chips. You are now betting 'off' amounts.

Look at the number of alternate bets you can make with the dollar chip grouped with the five dollar chip. Each of the following columns will signify an ongoing winning Series. The bets continue, as you continue to win in that series. Naturally if a loss occurs, you'd start a Series all over again.

Examples of running 'Series':

First bet:	$8	$8	$8	$7	$9
Second bet:	$5	$5	$5	$5	$5
Third bet:	$7	$6	$7	$7	$8
Fourth bet:	$10	$6	$9	$5	$10
Fifth bet:	$13	$9	$12	$8	$12
Sixth bet:	$11	$10	$15	$12	$7
Seventh bet:	$7	$11	$17	$12	$8

There is no end to the options you have. Betting 'off' amounts is a good move and a smart move — even if you're a high roller and mix in red $5 chips with your green $25 chips and black $100 chips.

The 'off amounts' give you so much flexibility, that all I want you to go is get the Theory of what it is and apply your own running series.

The examples I've shown you are just that: an idea of how to make each subsequent wager. The ones laid out for you are conservative, but you can make up your own, getting a little more aggressive — but not a crazy step-up in bets. Start slow until you get a cushion for allowing a higher Series to be applied.

This method of betting 'off amounts,' coupled with the

'Regression System' and utilizing my 'Up and Pull' money management, will solidify gambling Sessions.

If I were you — I'd backtrack and reread this whole section, chapter by chapter, until you understood it...these are your winning keys.

95

VARIATIONS OF REGRESSION

You already know the basic regression series of $10, $5, $10, $15, $20, $25 and the repeat $10, $5, $10, $15, $15, $20, $25.

I'm gonna give you a couple more variations, or you can come up with your own. These 'Series' are all based on winning each hand. A loss signals the end of that 'Session' and you start another one:

THREE DOLLAR TABLE

	A	B	C	E	D	F
First bet:	$5	$5	$6	$7	$6	$7
Second bet:	$3	$3	$3	$3	$3	$3
Third bet:	$6	$5	$4	$5	$7	$4
Fourth bet:	$9	$7	$7	$8	$12	$8
Fifth bet:	$12	$8	$9	$13	$6	$12
Sixth bet:	$15	$9	$5	$18	$10	$16
Seventh bet:	$20	$10	$10	$25	$15	$20

That's an easy chart to understand. Notice that they are mostly conservative, with B and C showing $10 as the maximum wager. If I were to choose the one you might like the best, it'd be either A or E. You can see that E uses a double Regression. Move over now to a $5 table.

FIVE DOLLAR TABLE

	A	B	C	E	D	F
First bet:	$10	$10	$8	$8	$7	$6
Second bet:	$5	$5	$5	$5	$5	$5

Third bet:	$7	$10	$7	$7	$8	$7
Fourth bet:	$12	$10	$11	$10	$13	$10
Fifth bet:	$15	$15	$16	$12	$18	$15
Sixth bet:	$20	$15	$20	$5	$23	$15
Seventh bet:	$25	$20	$30	$10	$28	$25

Notice that there are a couple of series that begin with an off amount. This is the point I'm trying to bring into your heads. In only one group did I go as high as $30 as my seventh bet (C). I believe that five times the amount of the table minimum is enough for a person with a $150 starting Series amount. You higher bettors can make your own aggressive set of wagers, but be sure you have a Regression in it and be sure the seventh bet is no higher than $50. Moving on to the ten dollar table:

TEN DOLLAR TABLE

	A	B	C	E	D	F
First bet:	$15	$15	$13	$13	$14	$15
Second bet:	$10	$10	$10	$10	$10	$10
Third bet:	$15	$13	$12	$15	$10	$15
Fourth bet:	$15	$20	$17	$10	$15	$20
Fifth bet:	$20	$27	$22	$15	$15	$30
Sixth bet:	$25	$34	$15	$10	$20	$40
Seventh bet:	$35	$40	$25	$15	$20	$50

Using off amounts at a $10 table, there are thousands of combinations that you can use, with double and triple repeats double and triple Regression amounts and variations of both five dollar increments and off-amounts.

Perhaps the one that might interest most $10 players is (F). It's aggressive and will kick off a nice return. Just for smiles, take (F) and rearrange the Series to put in another Regression about the fifth bet. Now see how you like it.

Okay, now we move on to the twenty five dollar table. However, first of all you must check out the chapter entitled "Session minimums," which is coming up shortly. It tells you how much you can take to each table, based on your starting Bankroll. No exceptions.

TWENTY FIVE DOLLAR TABLE

	A	B	C	E	D	F
First bet:	$30	$30	$35	$35	$40	$50
Second bet:	$25	$25	$25	$25	$25	$25
Third bet:	$25	$30	$35	$40	$30	$35
Fourth bet:	$30	$40	$50	$60	$45	$50
Fifth bet:	$45	$40	$65	$75	$60	$75
Sixth bet:	$60	$50	$50	$50	$75	$100
Seventh bet:	$75	$40	$35	$75	$90	$75

As you go higher in the betting series, the more opportunities for variations will open. Once you decide on a Series however, you can't change in mid-stream. Don't forget you still have to tie this in with the count, the side count of aces and your Bankroll. Finally we go to the $100 table, where only a scant few should go, based on that chapter called "Session Minimums:"

ONE HUNDRED DOLLAR TABLE

	A	B	C	E	D	F
First bet:	$125	$125	$150	$150	$140	$150
Second bet:	$100	$100	$100	$100	$100	$100
Third bet:	$100	$135	$125	$125	$140	$150
Fourth bet:	$150	$160	$150	$150	$165	$200
Fifth bet:	$200	$200	$175	$100	$175	$250
Sixth bet:	$250	$150	$200	$125	$200	$300
Seventh bet:	$300	$100	$225	$150	$250	$400

Since a Session at a $100 table must encompass an amount of chips of at least $3000, it should discourage you guys that play at this size table with a $300 roll, six cups of quarters, a handful of fifty cent pieces and a book of trading stamps. I am probably talking to only a few patrons who can play at this level. Same goes for you, as it does for the five dollar bettor. Set your Series in advance and stick to it.

That gives you a few ideas of how to handle winning Series, but I'd really like to see you come up with your own set. Something that you feel comfortable with, even a mix of two or three of my Series.

Most of all, I want you to stick to whatever predetermined Series you set. The temptation will be to make adjustments along the way. Don't!

The charts I've given you in this chapter are based on a neutral or poor deck. As you grasp the Theory behind the power of richness and poorness in a shoe, you will learn how to increase your opening Series bet and subsequent bets in a Series — based on the richness of that shoe.

I'll say it again. I do NOT use the richness of a shoe to accelerate my bets to astronomical amounts. I realize this is in direct contrast to other teachings, but it is the way I feel.

When the deck is rich, there is nothing wrong with a slight increase in your wagers, but keep a level-headed approach. You five dollar bettors lose an $80 bet, even if the deck is very, very rich at 75, and half of you will be forming lynch mobs with me as the guest of honor. Knowledge of the imbalance of tens in that shoe is a powerful tool, but it doesn't spit out guaranteed victories or even probable winning hands. It is just a vehicle to improve your play. Please heed these words.

The next chapter will give you some tips along the lines of 'soft' increases, but I'm more interested in you having this chapter be your guide to the running Series.

Mark this chapter — it will become a constant source of review.

96

SOFT INCREASES

The previous chapter gave you some examples of bets in a 'Series.' Each 'Series' started with the same amount. After a loss, that 'Series' was ended and the next 'Series' would again revert to that same starting amount.

It was explained to you that the examples were based on the shoe being at a neutral point and that is for anyone who is not a card counter.

Each 'Series' should start with the same amount as the prior 'Series,' although you have the option of dropping the amount of the first bet if you so desire.

I just heard X. P. Lane say to his wife that he'd like me to explain that last paragraph.

OK, go back to the previous chapter on Variations of Regression and look at the $5 chart: line C. The Series goes: $8, $5, $7, $11, $16, $20, $30.

Let's suppose you're in a losing streak and wish to lower the amount of your first bet. You could make your Series read: $7, $5, $6, $10, $15, $18, $25 or $6, $5, $7, $9, $14, $12, $15. The options are yours, as long as you leave room to regress after the first bet.

Please understand that the option to lessen your bet when you're in a cold run is a super smart move, not a stupid play.

If you go to a $5 table with a $200 buy-in, you could start your Series $8, $5, $7, $10, etc. If you lose the first hand (the $8 bet), twice in a row, your third Series could begin at $7. If that also loses, the fourth Series begins at $6.

I've already gone over that move in a prior chapter, but it is an important piece of information, as it harps on minimizing losses.

I hope X. P. Lane now grasps the message that is intended. It is a series of small moves — designed to accomplish the ultimate feat — To Win!!

Let's get to the soft increases. This is a method of starting your Series — based on the running count. There will be variations off of the running count, which will key your increasing the 'Series' bets by $1, to compensate for the count starting to climb.

Let's say you've bought in at a table and the shoe was just starting. You've decided on a Series string of $8, $5, $7, $11, $15, $20, $30.

Based on a six deck game, the count will start at 25 and each Series will begin at $8. When the count reaches 35, increase the amount of each starting 'Series' and continue: $9, $6, $8, $12, $16, $21, $31.

You've increased the amount of each bet in a Series by $1 to take advantage of the count starting to climb. An aggressive player could get a little heavier and use a more advanced pattern when he reaches 35.

For example: $9, $6, $9, $13, $18, $23, $33. On that sequence you had one dollar increases on the first two wins, two dollar increases on the third and fourth wins and three dollar increases thereafter.

Let's just go over what you're trying to accomplish. As the count begins to climb, you start to increase your bets over the basic Series amounts that were predetermined.

This way, you keep your senses sharp and begin to key on the changes in the running count. The amounts you set are your decision alone, but I want them to be consistent.

I hope you realize that it is impossible to give you four

thousand three hundred and fifty two variations of bets, when you use this method of increasing your Series bets as the count rises. The examples should give you enough insight into the point I'm trying to make. It is a very easy and effective way of shifting your bets up higher (in a conservative, controlled way), yet not making stupid, gigantic increases in your wagers.

Next we'll get into variations of bets based on the count. Begin with 35 being the first step in this soft increase. In the beginning of the chapter I showed you how to increase your running Series when you got to the count of 35. Here is one more variation: $9, $6, $9, $14, $19, $25, $36. In this case, we increased each bet as follows: one dollar, one dollar, two dollars, three dollars, four dollars, five dollars, six dollars. This is an increase over the basic 8-5-7-11-15-20-30. Notice the increases are small, but at least you're going up a little.

This is not as complicated as you might think. It is simply setting guidelines along your 'running count,' where you swing into your advanced betting process. Thirty five is the first point of increase.

I think X. P. Lane just looked over at his wife again. If he did, or if any of you did, go back and start reading the chapters until you have full grasp.

97

VARIATIONS OF SOFT INCREASES

I've given you a very basic move of increasing your Series bets, when the count reaches 35. You might make 30 your variation point, or 36 or 40. You may increase your running Series by two or three dollars per bet, based on an $8 starting wager. Just be patient and get the Theory.

I have zeroed in on one and two dollar increases off of the five dollar basic bet. As you get to play at ten dollar and twenty five dollar tables, the soft increases may be even six, seven, or eight dollars per bet.

The upcoming chart will give some examples of increases at a $10 table, where the basic Series was $15, $10, $15, $20, $25, $25, $40, $50. When the count reaches 35 and keeps climbing, the Series will start with a higher amount and continual adjustments are made in each succeeding winning wager. Remember, this is an increase in the above running Series:

    a) $17, $12, $18, $23, $29, $29, $45, $55,

    b) $16, $11, $17, $22, $28, $28, $43, $53.

Moving to the $25 table, we'll set a basic Series at $50, $25, $40, $50, $50, $75, $100, and again have our key be the point of 35.

    a) $55, $30, $45, $60, $60, $90, $115,

    b) $55, $30, $50, $60, $60, $90, $125.

You could even incorporate white chips at the $25 table, to give you more flexibility in adjusting your Series bets. Take a few minutes out right now to set up your own

Series, whether it be at the five, ten or twenty five dollar table.

Don't forget...this is strictly an option move that you can work into your game when the count reaches 35. With the last sentence still fresh in your mind, move right into the next chapter, before the thought disappears.

98

OPTIONS OF THE SOFT INCREASE

The last couple of chapters explained how to increase your Series bets in small amounts (soft increases), when the count reaches 35.

I hope you've grasped the full impact of making these adjustments at the count of 35, cause now I'm gonna vary the play.

I told you to use that number to make your soft increase. That is a number that I use and does not necessarily have to be the one you use. You could use 38, 40, 42, or 45 as your point of increase.

X. P. Lane's wife just ran out of the house screaming her head off. Now he realizes how important it was for him to understand each point I was making as we went along. And it was laid out for you in super simple terms.

Before your head also starts spinning, look at how simple this Theory is. I am trying to get you to get in the habit of taking advantage of the deck getting rich, but only in small betting increments.

Thirty five is on the way to a 'rich' point and a good time to start your soft increases. If you decide to wait until your 'running count' hits 40, that too is okay. But to get started in a disciplined approach, use my method. Don't forget that we're still keeping an eye peeled to that discard, tray and that'll be a big influence on our betting variations.

If you use 35 to start your soft increases of $1 per bet,

you could make another adjustment at the point of 40, since now we're getting even richer in our count. When we get to 40, another dollar could be added to both the starting Series amount and each subsequent winning bet in that 'Series.'

Suppose you have three points along your 'running count' where increases will be made. Those points could be 35, 40 and 45. Each time you reach that point, you will add your soft increases of one dollar, two dollars or three dollars, to take advantage of the rising count. Then when you get to the 'rich' designation of 49, the increases can become a little heavier. That'll be coming up in the next few chapters, but first get to understand the Theory of soft increases.

I've explained this to X. P. Lane is such a way that I think he is starting to see the light. You see all the trouble he could have saved himself, if he was just following my suggestions along the way and rereading the parts he couldn't understand? Hope you're not one of those guys that think you can get the entire method of card counting in one quick reading.

You can't. It takes a persistant desire to want to win, to absorb all the tiny things it takes to be a perfect player. That's what I wanna make you.

99

MULTIPLE SOFT INCREASES

Now don't go getting all unravelled at the prospect of having to memorize another variation. The soft increases at the count of 40 are perfectly acceptable. BUT — for you people who will devour this system in a matter of months and be looking for stronger off-shoots, let me introduce you to the method I use.

I'm not going into a long drawn out explanation of this, cause you should have absorbed the Theory by now. This adaptation will take very little explanation.

I will base the method at a $5 table, as that is what the majority of people in a casino really bet.

You wanna apply it to your higher tables, go ahead. Your increases can be in line with whatever Series makes you feel comfortable. Most important part is that you play with the right amount of Session money, which is 30 times the table minimum.

Okay, we're at a $5 table and you've laid out your Series in your head. It'll be $8, $5, $8, $12, $12, $15, $20. We'll be at a six deck game, count starting at 25.

As long as the count stays between 20 and 30, my Series bets will begin with $8. When the count reaches 19 and lower, the Series will begin with $7. So far that's easy to understand.

My increases are not based on getting to 35 or 40. They will come earlier and be multi-adjustable, based on the number of decks remaining in the shoe, which indicates a stronger count when there are only a few cards left to be played.

You know by now that a count of 40 with one deck remaining, is stronger than if the count was 40 with three decks left.

As the count climbs, the following increases are made:

Count reaches 31 . . . . Series starts with $9.
Count reaches 35 . . . . Series starts with $10.
Count reaches 38 . . . . Series starts with $11.
Count reaches 40 . . . . Series starts with $12.
Count reaches 45 . . . . Series starts with $13.
Count reaches 47 . . . . Series starts with $14.
Count reaches 49 . . . . Series starts with $15.

Did the light click on? I think so. Naturally there are multiple variations, based on the remaining decks and these moves you will have predetermined in your mind.

After you have mastered the soft increases at the count of 35 or 40, you can then move into these multiple moves or set up your own. Just a quick refresher. These are 4 different options you have:

a) Let 35 or 40 be the point in your 'running count' where you apply a small 'soft increase,'

b) Use the chart I've just laid out for you, whereby you have several points where the 'soft increase' will be used,

c) Rearrange your own amount of 'soft increases' and apply them to either (a) or (b) above,

d) Finally, you may not want to incorporate 'soft increases' into your betting Series. Perhaps you wanna wait until count reaches 49 (rich), and then you will start putting in increases. Good, that's your choice.

If you do incorporate a new 'soft increase' to your

'running series,' when it reaches a predetermined number, be sure that you add a certain amount to each subsequent follow up bet in that 'Series.'

Cause if you feel it is warranted to increase the first bet in a Series, it's only logical to assume that each succeeding bet deserves the same treatment. Go back a few chapters to where I gave you some examples to use, whereby you added either one dollar, two dollars, or three dollars to the subsequent winning bets in a hot Series. Set it up now, for the points whereby you will jump the amount of the first bet.

If you so desire, you could keep the increases at the same amount. In other words, suppose 30 was the key number for starting your next Series at $9, instead of $8. Every bet in that Series could be one dollar higher than the amount you preset for that Series.

My examples in that previous chapter gave you a couple of variables, such as two increases at one dollar, then two at two dollars then two at three dollars. You decide.

100

USING THE PLUS ACE COUNT

Now we slide into a sort of consolidation process. Still fresh in our minds is the matter of 'soft increases,' where we raise our bets as the 'running count' climbs. Let's not forget the additional chips to be wagered, when we get a shoe that has a plus count in aces to be dealt. It's time to incorporate that Knowledge into our bets.

Just for a refresher, go back and reread the chapters on side count of aces. They showed you how to easily keep track of the amount of aces that had been dealt, in comparison to the number of decks that still have to come out.

When you get that information, you gotta take advantage of it. This is the formula I advise. As the amount of aces remaining in the shoe increases, our chances of getting those aces has increased, along with our chances of getting Blackjack, cause there are more aces to help us.

As soon as you reach a plus 3 with the aces, regardless of how many decks remain in that shoe, you'll want to tag on to that imbalance. You do that by increasing your bet.

Suppose three half decks have been dealt and only 3 aces showed. There are three extra aces banging around in that shoe.

Immediately add $1 to your present bet. When it reaches plus 4 aces, go up by two dollars. When it reaches plus 5, it goes up three dollars per bet. And so on. Remember, we're at a $5 table and you're talking about 20% and 40% increases.

I can just hear my friend Imus Pressit groaning about the fact that I don't tell you to bang it a couple of green chips when this imbalance appears. He oughta press his empty head into the Discipline sections of my books to find out what gambling is all about.

Don't be like the Imus Pressit characters in the casino. They feel that any bet that doesn't put you on the brink of financial disaster is just a sissy wager. These guys go home crying every day. Gradual increases in your betting Series, is the proper way to handle these 'soft increases.'

If you reach the last playable deck in the shoe and the plus count on aces is two or more, double your unit increases.

That means if you're increasing your bets by one dollar, make it two. If you're at a ten or twenty five dollar table and increasing your bets by three dollars, make it six. You get the drift.

Now you're in an excellent position of getting an ace. If the deck is also rich at this time, triple your betting increases, cause the rich count and a plus in aces is the point you're looking for. Great chance Blackjack will come and you've got just as much chance of getting it as the other players at that table.

Notice I didn't say triple the size of your base bet — only the increases for the side count of aces, which have now reached the plus designation.

There will be days when you'll have a 'rich' count, coupled with a high plus of aces and the Blackjacks will just flow. Everybody else at that table will think it's just a matter of luck, but it ain't.

When that time does come, you wanna be able to take advantage of it. Now you can.

Remember way, way back at the beginning of the

book, where I stressed speed and harped on you to master card recognition? Now you can see how it all ties together. If you are lightning fast, you can use your free time to perfect the counting of aces. Applying both the 'running count' and the side count of aces into a strong amount of information that bang out extra wins.

Being able to utilize the speed factors I pushed at you, will give you time to do these other things.

101

WRAPPING UP REGRESSION

I live and die by the Regression System. If you don't catch the Theory of it, go back and study it again. The Regression offsets a chopping table and while the returns may be small, they'll be consistent. That's what gambling is all about: Winning!!

Lend me your ears for a moment, while we tie together all the pieces of the Regression System, as applied to card counting.

The object in counting is to reach the 'rich' designation. I give you points along the way where you can increase your 'Series' bets. You know that already.

The one thing that worries me about your play, is the fact that you don't fully grasp the 'Theory' of the Series. There's a chapter dedicated to this subject back in the Bankroll section.

The first bet at a table ignites a 'Series' and each winning hand means that 'Series' is still alive. A loss ends a 'Series' and the next hand starts a new one all over again.

I start my 'Series' bet higher than the table minimum, in order to be able to regress my bet back down to that minimum, thereby locking up a profit.

At a $5 table, you may start a 'Series' at either $6, $7, $8, $9, $10, etc. and then go back down to an amount lower than that initial bet. This is all laid out for you in previous chapters, so please back track and absorb that information.

The Theory behind the Regression is to get you in the

habit of winning. I hope you take the time to set up a 'Series' of bets that make you feel the most comfortable — as long as it's in line with your starting Bankroll.

In capsule:

a) Buy in at a table,

b) Continue your count (let's assume you were back-counting),

c) Have your Series pre-determined,

d) Begin your play with designated bet,

e) Keep your 'running count' accurate,

f) Keep your side count of aces accurate,

g) Add your 'soft increases' to your bet as count climbs,

h) If count starts to suddenly drop, don't be afraid to start reducing your 'Series' bets,

i) Keep eye peeled to Discard Tray so you know balance of decks still to be played,

j) Watch the dealer's up-card, to make sure he doesn't slide into pattern of turning over predominance of 'power-cards,'

k) Have 'Loss Limits' and 'Win Goals' entrenched in your mind,

l) Know exactly at what point you will increase your 'Series' bets to take advantage of the count when it reaches 'rich,'

m) Don't be afraid to leave the table if count drops to 'poor,'

n) As to (m) above, if count is 'poor' and you are still holding your own, stay there,

o) As to (m) and (n) above, it is all right to reduce the amount of your starting 'Series' bets, as long as you keep winning — regardless of count. Example: $6 starting

'Series' bet is small enough to play, as long as Trend at that table continues.

I think you've got an idea how to handle the Regression and still apply it to your 'running count.'

102

GUARANTEE AND EXCESS

Money Management means knowing how to manage your money. Do you know that 7,643 people just read that sentence and a light went on in their pea brains: "Holy mackeral! — is that what Money Management is?"

I can't believe the number of jerks that play at tables and never really know how important it is to be able to control their bets.

In reality, they are in control of their destiny. Whether you win or lose at a table, depends on your ability to be able to manage the Session money you bring to that table and then tie it into your Win Goals and Loss Limits.

The chapters on 'Guarantee's' and 'Excesses' explains this in detail, but Duwitt Agen just looked at his wife and said: "Gee, I hope he explains it again." The guy probably lives on the same block as that other blockhead, X. P. Lane.

For those two guys and you other lazy bones who failed to grasp those two chapters, I'll do it one more time.

The Guarantee and the Excess are the two piles you will make with your chips when the Win Goal has been reached.

- a) Start Sessions with $200,
- b) Win Goal set at 20% ($40),
- c) Goal is reached,
- d) Divide goal in half,
- e) Half goes in Guarantee pile, half in Excess pile,
- f) Put $200 starting Session money in your

pocket and Guarantee ($20) in your pocket,

g) You're Guaranteed to leave that table a winner,

h) Play with the Excess,

i) Every subsequent winning Series is divided in half,

j) Half goes in your pocket, half stays with Excess,

k) You keep increasing the amount you're guaranteed to leave that table with,

l) You keep increasing the amount of the Excess that you have to play with,

m) When Excess starts to go, grab what you can and add it to your Guarantee,

n) You leave that table a winner,

o) If the amount of the Guarantee is the amount of the Win Goal you set for the day, BEFORE you entered the casino, based on your Bankroll, you are done for that day,

p) If you are still short of your Win Goal for that day, go to Session two.

Now do you understand it? Duwitt Agen just ran in the kitchen and kissed his wife (which he hadn't done in eight years), he was so happy that he finally got it. Now she was happy: "Do it again—do it again—Duwitt Agen!" she screamed.

Meanwhile, across the street, X. P. Lane fell off his chair. Finally, finally, finally he got it. It usually takes a lot of explaining to X. P. Lane to reach him. But when he gets it, it sinks in and I just reached him.

I hope I reached all of you by now, in the grasping of the handling of your Win Goal, by setting up your own Guarantees and Excess piles.

I think I feel a little better myself.

103

CONTROL

You ever hear of putting the cart before the horse? Course you have. The effect of that move will get you a lot of attention from anyone who sees it.

I'm trying to get your attention by explaining what Money Management or control really is. You'll notice I put this chapter deep into this section, long after I explained how to manage your money. Now I'll try to explain why you manage it.

Gambling has been running rampant in this country for years and is growing in popularity by leaps and bounds. Billions of dollars are wagered every day — by intelligent, sharp, successful, and shrewd people.

Yet 95% of these geniuses are dorks when it comes to gambling. Not because they are stupid, but because they play stupid. And that's a big difference.

As I write this chapter, I'm in Atlantic City, in a hotel room at Harrah's Marina and it's 5:13 a.m. I have just completed four and a half hours of play at Blackjack, where it took me five Sessions to win $675. That's a pretty good hourly rate, but in reality a tough grind.

I am thinking of a lecture I gave earlier that night in north Jersey, where a group of people attended, to learn about casino games.

It was a three hour lecture and in all honesty everyone was having a great time. The audience was very receptive and the questions were extremely intelligent. One of the topics, of course, was Money Management.

251

I saw a lot of relations of Knod N. Agree in attendance, as my every word was met by a constant nodding agreement from the listeners.

Notice how people agree with the fact that you need Money Management, but just can't seem to put it into their play. Anyhow, we had a great rapt on this subject and you could see that my message was beginning to sink in.

Then came the usual dissenter. A guy by the name of Ken got up and asked for the floor. He proceeded to tell me what a line of crap I was handing these people by telling them they should set their Win Goals and Loss Limits, divide their money into Sessions, preset Series bets, etc.

I told him that this was the only way to win at gambling and that if people did not practice Money Management, they would never win at gambling.

This loud mouth passed over my explanations as though I never even spoke. He insisted that I give him 5 minutes of uninterrupted feedback, to get his point across, since he was: "...so kind as to listen to my side for a couple of hours."

What could I say? Well, the venom poured out of his mouth in a typical explanation of a guy who has been clobbered in his gambling forays. In a nutshell he said:

1) You're supposed to lose at gambling,
2) Everybody loses at gambling,
3) Money Management is a figment of imagination,
4) I (me) do not have the right to tell these people how to gamble,
5) I was probably sent by the 'mob' to force people to gamble,
6) I did not have the 'right' to change peoples gambling habits,

7) Why don't I shut up trying to explain how to control money and let people just enjoy themselves gambling and 'leave us have our fun'...

As he was talking, you could see the people getting mad, restless and irritated at his ramblings. They did not agree that "...we should be allowed to lose if we want to." (7) above was the crusher.

As if by signal, the crowd exploded and almost as one, they rose and booed and jeered him into submission.

I didn't say a word, but I knew that the people in the audience had grasped what I was trying to get across to them about Money Management and controlling their Bankroll. When someone tried to tell them to go back to their stupid ways of playing — they resisted.

What a great feeling! What a great thing to see those people show their feelings towards Money Management. Ken, the mouth who roared, was completely taken aback. I don't think he expected that to happen. Neither did I.

In the beginning of his retaliation, I feared that his rantings would destroy the points I had made. But I was wrong (again). These people made me feel ten feet tall.

The lecture ended about a half hour later and the applause was absolutely deafening. I think they were cheering for themselves and each other. I know a lot of people were reached that night.

You could see the smiles of satisfaction on their faces as they left that hall.

Money Management — how to control your money — a process sorely lacking in most people who gamble, but a virtue probably practiced now, by a lot of people in the lecture that night.

I walked on air to my car...

104

RIDING TRENDS

A friend of mine, who has listened to me at many lectures and follows my rules of Money Management, gets bored by my constant repeating things, even though I tell her that it is done intentionally to get my point across.

She tells me that it still disgusts her and insists that people only have to be told something once to get the message.

By the way, her name is Rhee Repeatpete, but that's another story.

Right now let's get to her problem. If repeating things irritates you, look at how repeating things is what makes professional gamblers winners.

A professional does not guess on the outcome of a game of Blackjack, or poker hand, or crap game, or sports event. No, he does his homework and looks for the pattern of trends or streaks that a player or team might be in.

When he finds that trend, the sharp player will jump on the bandwagon and ride that streak, as long as the wins keep repeating themselves.

A hot trend is the only way to beat the enemy and that Trend has to be handled with sharp Money Management moves.

Here I go repeating myself again. Go back to the very first section in this book on 'Trends' and read it again. It's the ability of the smart player to handle these trends.

When the 'Trend' is against you — get outta there. When it's a good 'Trend,' make it count.

As for my friend Rhee Repeatpete, I I I promise promise promise to to to learn learn learn how how how to to to stop stop stop repeating repeating repeating myself myself myself...

105

MARTINGALE SYSTEM

I never met this guy Martingale, but his system of betting has been handed down for zillions of years. He's had more impact on gambling systems than Dolly Parton's had on the flat chested look.

Everyone who comes up with a betting method, quotes a portion of betting progression tied back to Mr. Martingale.

I ain't gonna spend a lot of time on it, cause its' Theory is based on the fact that something is 'due' to happen.

Bet $5 and if you lose, bet $10 cause you're 'due' to win. If that bet loses, go for $20, then $40, then $80. If you're still losing, don't give up cause you're 'due' to win (the system says!). So you bet $160, then $320, then $640.

Bang—you win and get back the $635 you lost, plus a whole $5 profit. Of course if you lost that bet, you'd be out $1275, but that's not supposed to bother you. Your next bet would be only $1280 and surely you'd win that one and grab that $5 profit.

If that one also went down, they tell you to just suck up your gut and slide $2560 on the table, cause eventually you 'have' to win. Or does the system say 'due' to win.

I am sick of hearing about this type betting — where you constantly double your wagers, figuring you're due to win.

Don't bet this way...Period, Exclamation mark!!

You got as much chance trying to convince me that this is the way to bet, as you have of convincing me that Dolly

Parton will be remembered for her sexy kneecaps and not her tremendous singing voice and great set of lungs...but that's another story.

106

1-2-2 SYSTEM

This is not the Martingale System. It is a method of betting that is more aggressive than the Regression, but still does not put you against the wall, in the event of three straight losses.

I call it the 1-2-2 and it's not difficult to understand. Based on $5 unit bets, your first wager is five dollars. If you lose, the next bet is $10. If you lose that bet, you come right back with another $10 bet.

That's it. If that third bet goes down you have two options. Either go back and start another Series of bets with $5 or leave that table. My opinion would be to take a hike.

You know that four straight losses at the beginning of a shoe signals an exit from that Session. If the four losses occur during the course of a 'Session,' you have the option of staying there, based on three things:

1) Dealer's up-cards.
2) Running count,
3) You haven't reached your Loss Limit.

All of those things enter into your decision, if you're in the middle of a protracted run.

If you lose all three bets, your deficit is only $25; bad, but not devastating. On the winning side of the ledger, we have the way you handle victories. When you win the first bet, you let it ride and bet the whole $10. On the second win, you have two options:

1) Bet $10 again,
2) Regress down to a $5 wager.

Both of these options kick off the result of a winning Series. If you follow (1) above, you're sure of a $5 profit, even if you lose that third bet. If you use (2) above and regress your wager, you're sure of a $10 profit, even if you lost the third wager.

I'll give you a couple of examples of running Series. See which one you might like to use:

	A	B	C	E	D	F	G
1st bet:	$5	$5	$5	$5	$5	$5	$5
2nd bet:	$10	$10	$10	$10	$10	$10	$10
3rd bet:	$10	$10	$10	$5	$5	$5	$8
4th bet:	$10	$15	$15	$10	$10	$10	$12
5th bet:	$20	$20	$25	$5	$20	$15	$15
6th bet:	$30	$25	$40	$10	$10	$25	$12
7th bet:	$40	$20	$55	$5	$20	$35	$14

Notice how some of those 'Series' used a repeat on bet #3 and some went to the Regression on bet #3. But all of them reverted to 'Up and Pull,' somewhere along the line.

I absolutely demand that each winning bet, in any game you play, revert to the matter of pulling back a profit from the previous win. You 'must' make each win kick off a profit for that 'Series.' The 'Up and Pull' method gives you multiple variations.

Take a glance at (g) and note that I used off-amounts and Regression on the third bet and incorporated 'off amounts' to subsequent wagers.

If you like this method, set up your own Series, adding in the Regression and 'off amounts,' making use of the Up and Pull method.

A lot of aggressive players will like swinging into higher bets right away, so playing 1-2-2 will be right up their alley. Using the Theory of this method, your Bankroll will determine the level of your Series.

You could bet $10-$15-$15 or $10-$15-$20 or $10-$15-$5. All of those examples are the first three bets of a Series, all include the 'Theory' of the 1-2-2 and all of them hold down the total amount of outlay of money, while giving you the flexibility of multiple decisions.

Big thing to remember is that a loss signals the end of a 'Series' and you go back and start another one. If you had determined to use $5, $10, $10 as the increments you will use in that 'Series,' there is no deviating from it. The next 'Series' must use the same basic bets.

If you find yourself at a chopping table, naturally your 'Series' will kick off constant losses, since you'll win the first bet and, by letting it ride, end up with a loss. This is a pattern that the Regression System thrives on, as a chopping table at least kicks off consistent returns.

However, on tables where you have a lot of streaks, the 1-2-2 is very powerful. It gets you right into higher betting units and I know that is right down the alley of a lot of you swingers.

The next chapter will be an off shoot of variations, but first understand the basic concept of the 1-2-2 before moving on.

107

VARIATIONS OF 1-2-2

The following can be used at a $5 table, although the initial bets are set higher, to give some moves to the more aggressive player.

Notice that on these variation examples the second bet always rises one unit. After that, you have the decision to either regress, repeat previous bet, or continue to increase the next Series bet, while at the same time pulling back a profit (Up and Pull).

When a Series ends with a loss, the next Series begins with the same pattern, or is reduced by one unit. Following are some examples:

	A	B	C	E	D	F
First bet:	$10	$10	$10	$10	$10	$10
Second bet:	$15	$15	$15	$15	$15	$15
Third bet:	$15	$15	$5	$10	$20	$20
Fourth bet:	$5	$20	$10	$10	$20	$10
Fifth bet:	$15	$30	$15	$15	$30	$40
Sixth bet:	$25	$45	$20	$5	$30	$40
Seventh bet:	$35	$60	$25	$10	$40	$55

I am still an advocate of my own Regression System, but just like God made everybody different looking, he also made them different thinking. My system of conservative play may not be liked by every gambler, even if they apply their own Series.

This 1-2-2 method gives them a little more play in their Sessions.

108

ADJUSTING YOUR SERIES

Remember the amount of $50. For you conservative bettors, you'll like it. For you aggressive bettors, you'll complain. But you high rollers do a lot of yelling anyway, so just hold your britches for a second.

I want to give you a point in your betting, where you shift from conservative to aggressive 'Series' starts. That point is the amount of $50.

Shirley Goode is surely a good player. She enters the casino with her $450 and breaks it into three separate Sessions of $150 apiece.

She plays a good game of Blackjack and has mastered the strict rules of Money Management. Her only problem is that she doesn't know at what point she should start varying her starting bet per 'Series,' from conservative to aggressive.

This is the procedure for anyone from a $100 Session amount to $300. Start your Series in a small pattern, perhaps $7-$5-$8-$12-$15-$15-$20. Continue to use this 'Series,' until you reach a profit of $50 for that Session. As soon as that figure is reached, you can adjust your Series into a more advanced one, with $100 as the next point of change.

Shirley Goode hasn't been doing too badly this day and soon works her profit up to $50. At this point she will change her Series to read as follows. $9-$5-$12-$18-$23-$23-$30.

She will stay with this Series, as long as she keeps winning and doesn't drop under a profit of $50. If the tide turns and her profit goes under the $50, she must regress to the original Series of $7-$5-$8-etc.

However, if she keeps winning and hits the profit point of $100, she again adjusts her Series and shoots for the $150 mark.

Now her Series will read: $10-$5-$13-$19-$25-$25-$40. If she drops under $100 profit, she must revert to the second set of Series bets. If she keeps winning up to $150, another adjustment is made, again giving her a chance to go a little more aggressive.

In this instance you are setting points along the way, where the 'Series' can become higher. It is somewhat similar to the Theory on card counting, where you inject your 'soft increases' to the Series bets as the count rises.

Same way here. When Shirley has things going good and reaches a certain profit level, she will up her play.

When things go bad, Shirley Goode surely will have good adjustments ready to control her play and reduce her bets.

Setting these points along the route of your Session, will give you the keys to start making changes in a fraction of a second, at just the right time.

I hate to keep saying this, but the points made in this chapter are very important. Reread it.

109

THE AUTHOR AND MONEY MANAGEMENT

This section concentrates on Money Management. If you follow the systems that are laid out for you, or even pick up a spin-off of your own, you'll see a marked improvement in your play.

The single most important part of Money Managament is that it will minimize your losses. No amount of Knowledge will put you in a better position of winning more hands than the house.

So it behooves you to cut down your losses. When a Trend does pop, the betting systems show you how to take advantage of that streak.

Sounds simple, doesn't it? It is — but do you have the guts to perfect Money Management? It's up to you.

I was the smartest dope in the casinos when I first hit the scene in Vegas. I was a card counter before it became universally known and used a strong basic strategy approach to Blackjack. As far as Knowledge was concerned, I was a master.

As far as Money Management was concerned, I was a dope. There was no pattern to my bets, no systematic predetermined method of taking advantage of both short and long streaks.

My basic idea of betting was to 'let it all ride.' The only thought was how much I would win. It was that stupid approach that kept me broke, week after week.

Sure, I'd be ahead at various times during the day, but

the inevitable lack of control would eventually wipe me out.

Then I'd trudge over to the Greyhound bus terminal and grab a $1.50 ticket to Los Angeles. I could sleep on the bus and avoid having to pay for a motel room.

Eating was a snap. A pint of blood was worth a couple of donuts and a glass of juice. A two hour lecture in a California Bible school always ended up with a piece of pie and hot chocolate. On cold days you got soup. You know how many times I prayed for snow in July? I know God heard my prayers. But he used to whisper back to me: "Go get a job."

I knew every supermarket where a sales person would be introducing a new product and offering free samples. The days they gave soap powder and dog food were blanks, but sometimes they'd have cookies, fruit or ice cream.

A mall opening was a bonanza. Some stores would offer cheese, others pastry, others cocktail hot dogs and so on.

One particular opening had a deli, giving miniature sandwiches of different types of meat. I went back five times. Once with a jacket, once without, once with a hat, once no shirt, once with a borrowed hat. Each time I'd try to look bored or disinterested. I used to whistle or hum, to cover up the hungry growling in my stomach.

Finally the guy with the sandwiches said to me: "Hey Mac, sure you don't want a doggie bag?"

Since I had even less ego than money, I replied: "Sure, I'll have a couple to go. Can I take my pick?"

Remember, this is from a guy who maybe six hours earlier had $2000 in chips sitting in front of him.

I was a stupid player because of the lack of Money

Management. If I never learned Discipline or control, I'd still be running around accepting hand-outs or heaven forbid — working for a living.

I ain't trying to make you a professional gambler, only a smart player. I'm trying to make you realize how important it is to master these techniques of control.

The difference in winning and losing came to me — only after I grew up and stopped being such a dope. As I reflect back on those times, there is one thing that does stand out. When you're as broke and hungry as I was in those days, it always seemed that the donuts and coffee tasted so much better.

Today I buy my donuts and coffee, and while they still taste good, the thrill of winning consistently tastes even better.

Take a bite...

110
WRAPPING UP MONEY MANAGEMENT

Everytime I get to the point where a lecture or class or book or Seminar has to be consolidated into a wrap-up of Money Management, I fear that something will be left out.

Since this part of the Big 4 is so important, I suggest you re-read the chapters that you have some doubt about and then glance down this list of items and make mental notes of how you will apply each of them:

a) Set your Bankroll,

b) Divide Bankroll into Sessions,

c) Must have at least 30 times amount of table minimum,

d) Pick System you will use:

    1) Regression,

    2) 1-2-2,

    3) Your own method.

e) Set Win Goal,

f) Set Loss Limit,

g) If lose first four hands at that Session — leave,

h) When Loss Limit comes, or even if you're approaching it, get outa there,

i) When Win Goal is reached, break Goal in half,

j) Half goes in your pocket, along with your starting Session amount. That half is called your Guarantee,

k) Half stays on the table. This is called your Excess,

l)   Every subsequent win is broken in half,
     1) One half with the Guarantee,
     2) One half with the Excess.

m) When Excess starts to dwindle, grab what's left and put it with your Guarantee and *leave* that table,

n) If amount of the Guarantee at the Session was the Win Goal you set for that whole day, you're done betting — period,

o) If the profit at that Session is not the total of your original Win Goal, you may — if you wish — go to another Session,

p) Predetermine your pattern of 'Series' bets,

q) Do not deviate from 'Series' pattern,

r) Adjust 'soft increases' to your 'Series,' based on 'running count,'

s) Adjust 'soft increases' to your 'Series,' based on plus count of aces,

t) Adjust 'soft decreases' to your 'Series,' if side count of aces registers 'poor.'

All of these points were dealt with previously and I beg you to grasp their importance. Gambling is a rough undertaking, but the application of a strong Money Management method will give you a great start towards consistent winning days.

I hope nothing was left out of this summation and hope you'll heed these repititious words of wisdom.

They can only help you...

You know what's coming next...Discipline. Be sure you have all the information digested, before you start on the final leg.

DISCIPLINE 111

DISCIPLINE

We swing into the final stages of counting and glide into the part of the Big 4 that is the single biggest obstacle in the path of consistent winning days. The last and most difficult part of the Big 4 is Discipline.

The reason it's so difficult is that no one wants to follow the rules. Everyone knows it's the key to winning and everyone promises to practice it, but saying it and doing it are two different matters.

If you absorbed all of the messages that were passed on to you throughout the sections of Bankroll, Knowledge of the Game and Money Management, you'd have seen how they rely on each other to reach the ultimate goal — winning.

However, each part of the Big 4 is useless by itself. My friend X. S. Kash is a prime example. He has so much money that even God approached him for a loan when He was planning to renovate Heaven.

Anyhow, X. S. Kash has one weakness: he loves to play Blackjack. But even with all his money, he has yet to have a winning day. He doesn't know how to bet. So having money to play with is not your answer, although some guys think that a big roll guarantees constant returns.

Same is true when you lack money and can count a deck of cards in 3½ seconds. If you don't have money to bet, you can't play. Ninety percent of the people who gamble, lack at least one part of the Big 4 and that is too much to overcome. You must have the whole batch, in order to compete and hope to win.

Discipline is in the same family as the other three. If you ain't gonna follow the rules I lay down for you, then the other 3 parts won't mean diddly dang. Just take 5 minutes out of your hectic day, to dwell on each of these items in the Big 4. It is so easy to see how each of them offers something, towards getting you to the pinnacle of success.

Eventually the art of winning will always end up with the player himself. If you wanna win, you gotta perfect Discipline. It's so unbelievably hard to do this, but it sure beats leaving the casino in a rotten mood, time after time after time.

I told you earlier that 70% of the people who gamble, are ahead at one time during the course of their day, based on their starting Bankroll. But 90% of that 70% kick it back to the house. Why? Cause they're dopes...

I. M. Tite is running a little low on funds and has a tough time scraping together enough change to buy the daily paper. But he won't stop gambling.

Eventually he saves $100 that he takes to the casino and recites the Rosary eleven times on the bus, praying for just a small $30 or $40 profit.

On this particular day he catches an ice cold dealer and runs his winnings up to $200. He hasn't seen bread like this since he got lost in a bakery, back when he was four years old.

Do you think this dork will take his profit and run? No way!!! I. M. Tite becomes I. M. Nuts and starts upping his bets. Pretty soon his $200 profit, plus his $100 Bankroll, are a thing of the past.

He is wiped out and the ride home is like the death march from Battaan. He wants to die. Way, way, way, way back in his mind he knows he done wrong. But he won't admit it. He's too busy blaming bad cards, bad luck, rotten players at the table, and lucky dealers.

You know who he should blame? No one but himself. He has no Discipline and no right to be gambling. His next trip will be no different. The results are always the same. He'll never stop going for the kill.

How about you? You got Discipline? If you don't...get it or you'll never win at gambling.

Discipline is an art. It takes guts to discipline yourself. If you ain't got Discipline and don't even have the guts to force yourself to practice control of some type, then I sure as heck can't help you.

Telling you that you need Discipline won't do the trick. You gotta suck up your gut and Learn How to Win.

112

LEARN HOW TO WIN

This isn't an idle statement, nor is it merely four words strung together. The message tells you exactly what gambling is all about. You must **Learn How To Win.**

I found that the easiest way to do that was to accept smaller returns, but on a more consistent basis. I choose this 'Theory' over the one that says you should go for the big kill. You know who usually ends up getting killed? It ain't the casinos baby!

Half of you big geniuses reading this page just shook your head in disgust. You don't want the small return. You wanna go for the six figure paydays that you dream about.

That's all they are man, dreams. It's a silly notion passed down through the years, that gambling is supposed to be the road to riches. That's gobblety gook.

You know how many people tell me: "Man, you must be rich, you know so much about gambling." I tell them that just knowing how to play is not enough, that there are other facets involved in winning.

But they just give me that 'knowing smile,' the sly wink that indicates they don't buy that explanation.

Well you better buy it, cause it's the truth. All my Knowledge gives me no more than a 50-50 chance of winning.

To inch myself ahead of the house, I rely on the Money Management systems I've perfected. These methods, coupled with a strong Disciplined approach, have allowed me to minimize losses and take advantage of hot Trends.

However, I believe my most important attribute is the acceptance of small wins, rather than going for the big payday.

Suppose I drove three hours to Atlantic City with $2000 as my starting Bankroll and was all set to go up to a table. If a representative of that casino stopped me and said: "You can go and play and try to win your 10% or 20%, or I'll hand you a guaranteed $75 payoff right now and you must go home."

Without a moment's hesitation I'd grab the $75. What would you do? The object of gambling is to win. The amount is irrelevent, because it is based on your Bankroll. You think gambling means you gotta win thousands and thousands of dollars. All you gotta do is win.

I've seen professional gamblers leave a casino with a $40 profit, after seven gruelling hours at the table and smile with a smug sort of confidence.

Next to him is Helen Bakk, an occasional craps player from North Jersey. She started with $200, ran it up to $800 and kicked it all back for a frustrating day at the tables. She is cursing, glaring, steaming mad. Helen looks like she's been to hell and back.

She has! Now she's suffering for it. She wasn't content to win within the boundaries of her Bankroll. She just liked the excitement of playing. She doesn't know how to win.

Now reality has hit her. She no longer has the $800 she was up, nor does she even have the deuce she started with.

She's never learned how to quit a winner. The pro has been there many times, both as a winner and a loser.

Winning small amounts is a lot better than losing. Or haven't you learned that yet? You got a lot to learn...

113

PERCENTAGE RETURN

You already know what a conservative player I am. If you're conservative too, you'll be easy to reach. If you're aggressive and want high percentage returns, you're gonna have a hard time accepting my suggestions.

I speak from years of experience. Some losing years, some winning ones. I can tell you that the frustration I felt during the bad times was so overwhelming, that I felt like I was being dumped on by everyone. You begin to feel like you're snake-bit.

Of course it isn't true, but you tend to feel that way, because of the constant losses. When I learned how to win, the feelings were so great that it turned my whole approach around. The wins were not gigantic, but they were wins nonetheless.

The trick was in the percentage returns I set. The lower the Win Goal, the more often it became a reality. All of a sudden I was picking up consistent wins, even though they were small.

If I took $500 to the casino and set a Win Goal of $100 (20%) it was a struggle, but not too difficult to achieve. With the same $500 and a goal of 10%, it seemed that I was closing in on my goal a lot quicker.

So I increased the amount of my Bankroll and reduced the amount of the goal. The Theory being that if it is fairly easy to win $50 with $500, then it is even easier to win $50 with $1000.

A lot of you high rollers are laughing up your sleeve,

but some of you are waiting for a logical explanation.

Let me see if I can put it in laymans terms. Since I use 20% as the Win Goal in all my books, let's stay with that percentage return.

Suppose you take $100 to the casino and I tell you to play until you win $5. You'd laugh in my face: "Are you kidding? You want me to win $5 and quit? Heck, winning $5 is a snap!"

Think how many times you've been ahead $5 in the casino, with a starting Bankroll of $100. Admittedly it is very easy to win that amount. Well, if it's so easy to win $5 with $100, why not take $1000 and play to win $50!! It's the same percentage. If that's too small for you, just add a zero to your Bankroll and bring $10,000 to battle. Play until you win $500.

If it's so easy to win $5 with $100, it's just as easy to win $500 with $10,000, cause it's the same percentage. And $500 winnings should get a lot of attention from you plungers. You'd like to haul that amount home with you on each trip.

But you won't bring $10,000 with you to win the $500 and yet you scoff at the same percentage return with a starting Bankroll of $100.

This is not a silly example. Roll it around in your head a few times and see it you can grasp what I'm driving at. A few chapters ago I stated that the more I bring, the less percentage return I go for and it makes a lot of sense.

Gambling is just about a 50-50 proposition. If the laws of probability were to fall exactly as they should, you would win approximately 49% of the hands you play and the house would win approximately 51%.

That means you're fighting games where the edge is not in your favor to win. How can you look for anything more than small logical returns? As soon as I get ahead, I've got one foot on the floor, my eye on the door and my heart begging my head to start the motor for a quick getaway.

The percentage return I suggest is 20%. That's based on the average Bankroll of $400 that people take to battle. If you take more, drop the amount of your Win Goal and get in the habit of accepting smaller wins.

114

HANDLING THE GOAL

You're gonna have a lot of trouble accepting my suggestions on percentage returns, but it is the only way to get in the habit of winning.

If you didn't skip over the first 80% of this book, you'd be aware that reaching your Win Goal is not the end of your day. If you have an over abundance of Discipline and reach a 20% profit, there are three options:

    a) Take your money and run,

    b) Utilize my Guarantee and Excess method,

    c) Be a dork and pour your profits back to the house.

These three options should be familiar to all of you. (c) is probably the most noticeable, as you've all walked the plank at least once in your life. (a) will be practiced by only the very, very, very smallest percentage of players. It's really rough to set a goal, reach it and then run for the exits. Maybe you'll say you'll do it, but I rather doubt it.

(b) is the one I want you to zero in on. It is soooo easy to understand and yet soooo hard to get you to do it. This is how I want you to handle your day:

    1) Set your Win Goal based on your Bankroll,

    2) Shoot for a 20% return,

    3) When goal is reached, break it in half,

    4) Immediately utilize method of Guarantee and Excess,

        a) Half in pocket called Guarantee,

        b) Half stays on table called Excess.

5) Every subsequent winning Series is divided between Guarantee and Excess,

6) Stay as long as Excess remains intact.

That's the 323rd time I've explained that method to you. If you can't grasp its' impact and the power of that move, then you ain't learned a thing about the art of Money Management.

This system is a disciplined application of locking up a profit and yet still keeping you in action when the Trends are in your favor.

I believe it is very easy to reach a logical Win Goal. It is the strong player than knows how to handle that goal when he gets there.

115

LOSING DAYS

Hey man, you're gonna have losing days in gambling, regardless of how good a counter you are, so don't think my method is gonna guarantee a 100% bonanza everytime you enter a casino.

Discipline doesn't just apply to the winning side of your Sessions. It also has to be put into play on the days you run into some hot dealers.

You know how hard it is to walk away from a game when you're winning. Well, it's even harder to walk when you're losing. You try to give yourself all kinds of reasons why you shouldn't retreat and look for another game:

a) You think your bad trends will end,
b) You won $300 at this table last month and think it's your lucky seat,
c) You ordered a drink and don't wanna disappoint the waitress by not being there,
d) You're too lazy to move.

All of the above could be applied to most people who suffer through a long losing Session. It is really rough to push your stool back and leave that table. I honestly think that most players believe that losing streaks are 'due' to change.

They're right, but who can tell how long that 'due' will last. Most times your reluctance to leave will do you in.

The chapter on Loss Limits covers exactly how you must handle losing Sessions. I suggest you review it.

Anyhow, here are some fine points:

- a) Set your Loss Limits before you begin,
- b) In Blackjack, the maximum Loss is 40%,
- c) You set whatever Limit makes you feel the most comfortable, as long as it isn't over the maximum,
- d) When things are going bad, have the intelligence to pack it in.

Sometimes I think it's harder to quit when you're losing then when you're winning, but it still comes under the heading of Discipline. It's being able to control your emotions and play only at winning Sessions that will eventually make you a powerful Blackjack player.

Handling yourself at losing tables is something you must learn to do. It ain't no disgrace to leave a game when that dealer suddenly starts pulling seven card twenty ones.

You know what gets me? The guy who loses 14 straight hands, finally drops his last two chips and turns to the guy on his left and jokingly says: "Well, guess this isn't my day. But what the heck, I had a good time!"

Good time????? The boob just lost $500 and thinks he had a good time!

Then he saunters away, acting like the $500 he blew doesn't really bother him. Silently he's planning on how to make up for the money he lost:

- a) Tell his wife he lost his wallet and can't go on the vacation they planned,
- b) Cut the tip on his paperboy from 50¢ to a quarter,
- c) Forget to give his kids their allowance,
- d) Bypass a couple of tolls on the Parkway,
- e) Cut down to 2 packs of butts a day,
- f) Ride his bike to the train 3 days a week to

save gas,

g) Skip taking the kids to the Saturday movies for a few weeks,

h) Play sick on the night he promised to take his wife to dinner.

All of a sudden his smile widens. The loss of that $500 isn't really going to hurt after all. It'll just take a little sacrifice on the part of the wife and kids. You think this is a fairy tale? I think it is a sad tale — but a true one.

I'm not saying you have to swallow poison every time you lose a few hands of Blackjack, but there are degrees of how bad a beating you have to take. When you're going bad on losing day, limit those losses. And don't act like losing doesn't bother you — you're only kidding yourself.

116

TOTAL CONCEPT

For a very good reason I have inserted this chapter in the Disciplne section, even though it ties in with Money Management. By putting it in this section, you will concentrate on it more and perhaps I'll feel confident that you understand my Theory of betting.

Based on the Regression method of wagering, I explained that there were points along your 'running count' whereby you would increase the amount of your 'Series' with soft increases. This is when the count reached certain points, such as 35 or 40, etc.

Of all the chapters in the book, the grasping of the 'soft increases' may be the hardest. I do it to take advantage of the 'running count' starting to climb and I do it with small increases of $1, or $2, or $3 at a time.

I also told you that I do NOT use card counting to make gigantic increases in my wagers, when the count reaches the 'rich' designation. But I'd like to touch on your moves at that 'rich' point.

Keeping in mind all of the explanations I gave you about 'soft increases,' swing that 'Theory' over to the moment when the deck becomes 'rich.' That moment is the count of 49. By checking the discard tray, you can now see how many decks are left to be played and how 'true' your count is.

Suppose the indication is that two or less decks remain. If you were using a 'Series' run of $8-5-7-12-15-15-20, you would swing into a $5 increase on the first and every subsequent bet of that 'Series.'

If a lot of decks remain, the increases would be $3 per bet. If the 'running count' dips beneath 49, revert to your original betting amounts. But let's say the count continues to climb. Use certain points to increase the amount of your starting 'Series' bet and every subsequent winning bet in that 'Series.'

Okay, let's say your count reaches 49 and only 2 decks remain to be played. Based on the above 'Series,' the bets would then read: $13-10-12-17-20-20-25. That's an increase of $5 per bet.

Suppose the count continues to climb. When it reaches 57, add another $5 per bet, beginning with the first bet of the 'Series.' Now it will read: $18-15-17-22-25-25-30.

Notice that you are only $10 per bet over the initial starting 'Series.' You are taking advantage of the climb in the count, but only to the tune of $10 per bet. That in itself is enough.

Don't forget, you are still using the Knowledge of that 'running count' to improve your basic strategy.

As the count continues to climb, keep raising your bets — but only at $5 a pop. The next key point is 65 and now the 'Series' reads: $23-20-22-27-30-30-35.

The shoe is 'very rich,' but based on your Session money, these are decent enough wagers to make. If you win, you'll feel very good. If you lose, it is not a fantastic dent in your Bankroll.

Continuing along, we'll say the count keeps rising and soon it hits the next level that calls for an increase. I use 8 ticks on the count to signal a jump. When it gets to 73, add another $5 per bet. Now your 'Series' reads: $28-25-27-32-35-35-40. I think you get the idea.

If the count starts to dip, you must begin keying on the lower bets per 'Series' and this is going to take a lot of Discipline. A lot of times there will be a big jump in the 'running count,' whereby the dealing of a single hand can change the designation between 'neutral' and 'rich' in the flick of an eye. You gotta concentrate and catch those fluxuations and immediately make an adjustment in your bets.

Also, when the shoe ends, your count naturally swings all the way back to 25, to begin the new come-out. Your betting 'Series' must drop all the way back to the original $8-5-7-12-15-15-20.

If you have a decent winning Session going at this time, you could then start your 'Series' a little higher and perhaps go to: $10-5-9-16-20-20-25. That's up to you. There are so many variations you can make.

Since this multiple amount of variables in both your count and your bets will require a tremendous amount of concentration, I put this chapter in the Discipline section.

It is going to take an awful lot of concentration and Discipline on your part to be able to make these moves in a fraction of an instant.

I know you can do it. It'll take some work on your part, but you'll get it. The results will be more than worth the effort.

Again I remind you that I merely give you an example of several betting 'Series.' It is a virtual impossibility to list the thousands of potential 'Series' that you could use. That part is very simple. Pick the 'Series' that best suits your Bankroll and your temperament. Or haven't I said that before...

This is another one of those reread chapters that will take a lot of referring back to. Mark the spot in your book.

117

IMPORTANCE OF CHARTING

I've already talked about charting a table in an earlier section and even referred back to it on numerous occasions. It is such an important part of your approach, that a little emphasis on this subject won't hurt you.

I ain't smart enough to understand why Trends happen, but you better zero in on the fact that streaks occur over and over in gambling. No one can explain why and I sure as heck ain't gonna try. But the casinos are living proof that streaks do occur.

Go to any table — any game — and watch a few hands. Watch how powerful and consistent the streaks are. A cold craps table will have 8 out of 10 shooters seven out. A Blackjack dealer will win seven hands in a row and then bust 6 straight times.

The color red will show in Roulette eight straight spins. Five straight players in Baccarat will deal five 'Bank' hands in a row before they show a 'Player' hand.

It goes on all day long. Trends dominate in gambling. When I finally got that thought through my thick skull, it was only a matter of time before I used these streaks to my advantage.

I go so far as to spend hours checking out tables, before risking one dime of my money.

In Blackjack I'm looking for everything to be in my favor before playing. Unless all of the following is running my way, I won't play:

     a)   Dealer showing predominance of small cards

as 'up card,'
b) Count is 'rich' or 'high neutral,'
c) Opening at first base at the table I'm charting,
d) Proper minimum amount at table, based on my Bankroll.

Sometimes it's so frustrating to find two or three of the above to be in my favor, but I never break the rules. If everything isn't there — I walk.

I want you to chart the tables and become a proficient back-counter before jumping into a game.

Remember old Etchy Pants and the stupid approach he had to the games? He'd jump up to the first stool he could find and start shoveling in his bets. This boob is obsessed with getting into action. He acts like the tables will disappear if he hasn't got both elbows pressed on them, 30 seconds after he arrives.

There's a girl I know (name deleted) who is a secretary for a very successful lawyer. She frequents the casinos often and when she tells her boss that she is going, he'll take a $100 bill and give it to her: "Play red on Roulette at the first table you come to!"

That's his system for playing. If she wins the $100, she brings the profit back to him. It's a one shot deal.

The first two times he won and smugly told me that he had conquered the game of Roulette. I told him it was probably the rottenest system I ever heard of.

Anyhow, the last 10 trips have resulted in 8 losses and 2 wins. This girl is afraid to tell him when she is going, as his mood has not been too chipper when she comes back and tells him he lost.

It isn't a bad system — it's a horrible one. Where do people come up with such nonsensical ideas? He has no idea of what type trend or streak that particular table that she will go to is in. There is no logic behind this play.

And don't act like you're lily pure! How many of you have given a buddy $10 to play a horse, or a couple of doubles at the track, when you were unable to go. You'd pick some cute names of the horses, or 'lucky' numbers for him to play for you.

Not one ounce of charting or handicapping went into that wager. And you're the same big spender that would out-fumble three other guys for a $2.25 tab at the morning coffee break.

Charting a game, to see which pattern is showing at a table, is an important part of your approach. It takes Discipline to leave a table when no solid plus streak is showing in your favor.

Charting a table is not a suggestion for helping you out. It's a MUST for the serious player.

118

THE PROFESSIONAL GAMBLER

One of the most irritating comments that is thrown at me during a lecture or TV show is always put in the form of a statement of fact. Some guy will call in and say: "Nobody can win at gambling! The house always wins!"

That is a stupid statement, uttered by a jerk who obviously doesn't have a thread of evidence to back up his erroneous ramblings.

To say 'nobody' wins at gambling is dead wrong. You'd be surprised how many professional gamblers there are in the country. People who grind out a living at either horse racing, sports, poker, craps, Blackjack, etc. run into the thousands.

Most pros are centered around Vegas, but Atlantic City also has a growing number. New York has a bushel of pros and their main game is the ponies. Some go for the flats, others for the trotters.

These people are experts in the game they concentrate on and it's interesting to note that some of them know little or nothing about another game. It's not uncommon to hear a professional horse player state that he's never seen the inside of a casino.

A dyed in the wool crap player thinks a 'hoarse' race is a contest between a group of people with sore throats.

That's because most pros concentrate on just one game — the one they're the best at. And you better believe they are 'great' at that game. That's due to the fact that every waking day is spent trying new methods, new systems, revising betting patterns and studying Trends.

Naturally, it's impossible to win every time, but a pro has brought his chances of losing to rock bottom.

I'm not trying to persuade you to become a professional gambler. I do want you to approach the game with the same intelligent outlook. That means disciplining yourself in the way you will control your bets and accept predetermined Win Goals and Loss Limits.

A pro bets to win — not to bet. A horse pro may bet on one race a day, or maybe one race in two days. The novice bets every race: win, place or show, trifectas, exacts, quinnellas and doubles. How the heck can this dope hope to conquer every race, when a pro, who is at the track every morning at 5 a.m. doing his homework, has trouble trying to find one horse per day to wager on?

Many times I'll drive two hours to the casinos, play for 20 minutes, pick up the days pay and head back home. I'm a perfect card counter, yet willing to play for only several minutes to accomplish my goal.

The idea is that my goal is to Win. The goal of the novice is to play.

I'll tell you one thing though. No matter how long I've been gambling and no matter how many good days I've had, there is one thing that always hurts — losing.

Any pro will admit the same thing. And you know where it hurts the most? Right in the gut, baby. Right there in the old solar plexus. Now I don't mean I wanna run out and leap into the path of a train when I lose, but it does hurt. It's at those moments that I wish I had a nice soft job painting the peak of the Empire State Building, or cutting the grass in a South Korean mine field.

But then a winning streak pops up and I forget the bad times. Point I'm trying to make is this:

1) Pick the game you understand the most,
2) Master it,
3) Have the Discipline of a Professional Gambler,
4) Set hard and fast Win Goals and Loss Limits,
5) Predetermine every single move you'll make,
6) Pay absolutely no heed at all to any outside input,
7) Be able to accept small wins,
8) Don't become a professional gambler.

Even if you're not a pro, you can surely use the disciplined approach that he practices.

The next time you hear a loudmouth say: "Nobody wins at gambling!" give him a sly wink and say a silent prayer for him. He's probably a professional loser...

119

THE LOUD MOUTH

Being in the casinos 4 days a week, for lo these umpteen years, gives me a first hand look at the thousands of people who venture into the world of gambling.

Are they characters? Man, Damon Runyon was an altar boy compared to some of the ding-a-lings that are let out of the cages, to meander around the casinos and shovel money to the enemy like it was poison. And then make dorks out of themselves while they're doing it.

I enjoy watching these people in action, although you can tell by the looks on the faces of the dealers, that the loud mouths would make their day, if they'd move to another game.

For some reason, which I cannot understand, these jerks think they have to act like a Big Shot at the tables. If 47 people don't turn and look at them during the course of the day, they think there's something wrong.

But how can you help but look at the loud mouth? There's no question you can hear him. His voice booms out every bet he makes, as though everyone in the casino was supposed to be interested in the outcome of every hand he plays.

As soon as he gets to the table he'll make himself known to all the other players. "Howdy friends, my name's Loud — I.M. Loud, from out west. Just wanna show you easterners how we play Blackjack out in God's country. You all have any questions about how to play, just ask old I. M. Don't mind sharing my talents with you good folks." ...and that's just the beginning.

He buys in for $500 and starts betting $25 a pop. Then he'll spot a little old lady at the table, minding her own business and betting $5 a hand. He'll proceed to make one of his obnoxious statements: 'Hey, little lady, why you betting only five dollars? Your hubby cut your allowance? Doesn't he know you gotta bet big to win big."

Naturally he says it loud enough to get the pit bosses attention. Then he'll roar laughing at his sadistic attempt at being friendly.

In the next 15 minutes this bore will break every etiquette rule in captivity and some that weren't even invented yet.

    a) He'll make suggestions to the guy on his right as to when he should hit or stand,

    b) Yell at the cocktail waitress for not being right there when he was ready for a drink,

    c) Scream at the player at 3rd base when he made a move that allowed the dealer to win the hand (the player at third base took a hit with a 15 vs the dealers ace).

    d) Ridicule the dealer for helping one of the other players at the table,

    e) Knock over a drink that belonged to the player on his left and then bellow out not to worry, cause the casinos water down the drinks anyhow,

    f) Light up a cigar that couldn't have cost more than $1.50 a gross and proceed to blow smoke in every direction.

No one is safe from the acid tongue of this mouth that roars. When his wife comes to the table, he gives her a handful of quarters and tells her to get lost at the slots.

Then he'll flip a $25 chip to the dealer and scream loud enough to drown out the din at two crap tables: "Here ya are Sonny, a green chip for your trouble. Guess old I. M. is the only person nice enough to tip ya." Then he'll remind the dealer that he duked him, every other hand for the next 30 minutes.

Pretty soon this boob gets his come-uppance. The dealer gets hot and bangs him eight hands in a row. With each loss, this boob gets nastier and nastier. He accuses the dealer of dealing from the bottom of the deck (they deal from a shoe). He screams that the house is crooked and there are shills at the table playing against him.

When he finally loses his wad, he slinks off into the crowd still mumbling and complaining, blaming everyone but himself.

I. M. Loud is a jerk. There are a lot just like him in every casino. The other players detest him. You've seen and heard them at every track, ball park and casino in the country. They don't even realize how stupid they make themselves look.

But the house people recognize the type and try to ignore them. They figure they'll eventually burn themselves.

The jerk brings his own matches...

120

EXPERT OR DOPE

I hinted at this before and was hoping to get past at least one of my books, without telling you from my heart what I think of people who gamble.

In reality I have absolutely no right to condemn any man or woman who gambles. That's their choice. They wanna bet the family jewels on the turn of a hand of Blackjack or spin of a Roulette wheel — that's their business.

I imagine 75% of the people in this country make some type of wager, on something or other, at least once during the course of a year. And 90% of those people probably bet at least once a week.

Gambling has captured the hearts of the rich and the poor, the old and the young. They love it, so who am I to condemn them for it.

If that was the case, I'd have to tar and feather my mother. She trudges to Atlantic City every other week, visits the local Churches for a session of Bingo at the very least 3 times a week and even sneaks in a few plays on the weekly lottery.

If you were to boil in oil every woman who played Bingo, the foreign countries who ship us the oil would reap trillions of dollars. In fact they'd probably run out of the gook.

I ain't condemning you for gambling. I'm condemning you for gambling when you don't fully understand the game you're risking your money on.

That brings us to a very sticky statement: 'Anyone who

gambles is an Expert or a Dope.' If you know every single solitary thing about the game you're playing, then you are an·Expert at it and have a decent chance of picking up some profits.

But if you are not perfect in the game of your choice and still wager money on it...then you're a Dope.

In gambling, there is nothing in between. If you do not know everything about the game you're betting on, you're courting disaster and no intelligent person would do that. Yet people bet every day with this gross lack of Knowledge.

How about you? What classification would you put yourself in? Expert or Dope!!!!

121
YOU, ME AND DISCIPLINE

I ain't no smarter than any of you people reading this book. The only thing I know is gambling. But that's because I work at it.

If I tried to do anything else, it would be a complete disaster. When it's my turn to start supper, my daughters have to leave me a 3 page typewritten set of instructions on how to boil water. So far this week I've done it right two times out of five. That's not bad. You should have seen my percentage when I first started. But I'll keep working at it.

I've also got to learn how to change flats on my car, cause it's very embarassing having my mother called out in the middle of the night to do it. Not that she doesn't do a good job, but the arthritis in her hands has slowed her down somewhat and I feel embarassed standing there and using a person who does not do a quick job. But she needs the buck and a half I slip her, so maybe I'll keep her on.

The point I'm trying to make is that my criticizing the way you gamble is right in line. Maybe it's the only thing I know how to do, but I do it well.

I'm positive that if you were to follow my strict rules of Money Management and Discipline, you'd start banging out some decent returns. I didn't say you'd become rich, but you would stop losing. Your losses, with the use of Loss Limits, would be tremendously minimized.

So what's the secret? Discipline, my friend, strictly Discipline.

The Bankroll you can acquire. The Knowledge you will

learn as you leaf through these pages. The Money Management is something you will pick up as you become more proficient in studying these approaches.

But Discipline takes a lot of control. It requires a fanatical desire to win. That I have! Discipline is all that separates your playing Session from mine. I sure do hope you realize the importance of it and acquire it.

Since I also want to improve myself in some other areas, I'm gonna really concentrate on that 'boiling water' problem tonight.

It's gonna take a lot of discipline on my part to concentrate and get it down pat. When I get it right, they don't make me do the dishes.

122

WRAPPING UP DISCIPLINE

This about brings us to the end of the Big 4. The section on Discipline is the smallest of all, but the message will make the biggest impact on your game.

In reality, the rest is up to you. If you really wanna win, you'll follow the complete set of rules I've laid out. It's gonna be doggone rough to play in such a controlled fashion, but the results will make up for the lack of thrills.

If I were to ask you to reread certain chapters in this book, the ones that jump into my mind right off, are as follows:

- a) Trends,
- b) Charting a table,
- c) Sessions,
- d) Series,
- e) Regression System,
- f) Variations of Regression,
- g) Up and Pull,
- h) Total Concept,
- i) Win Goals,
- j) Loss Limits.

These stand out as the ones having the greatest impact on your disciplined approach to gambling. They seem to be a notch ahead of the others, but of course everything has it's own impact into making you the perfect player.

Every teenie-weenie inch of an edge that you glomb from the other chapters, will help fill in the entire package of Learning How To Win.

After you Learn How To Win — I want you to retain these messages for as long as you intend to risk even one dime in a game of chance.

Perfecting Discipline is hard work baby, perhaps harder than anything you ever tried to conquer.

In fact, Discipline is probably as hard for you to master as boiling water is for me. But if you don't master it, you'll also be in hot water up to your eyeballs.

Take heed to these little messages I give you. In a very direct way I'm trying to get you to realize how important it is to have the Big 4, before you even dream of attacking a table.

It's your money, so learn how to protect it. You do that by becoming the perfect player, regardless of how often or how little you play.

So You Wanna Be A Gambler!!! Be the best...

FAST DEALER

In every casino you'll find a few dealers who think they're working against the clock. They're impressed with their ability to slide the cards out of the shoe in machine gun fashion.

Then they'll go right to the player at first base, trying to get him to make a quick decision. If the player was as perfect as I want you to be, you should be able to make that decision instantly, but that's not the point.

Most players just can't do it. This rude dealer has lost conception of what his job really is. He is impressed with his speed and is secretly hoping the casino bosses notice his dexterity. He is shooting for a promotion to floor person.

Who's the victim of this dealer's selfish plans for self improvement? It ain't Little Red Riding Hood, baby. It's you, the player, who must bear the brunt of this dork's showing off.

A sharp floor person will remind this dealer that he is going too fast and making it hard on the players, but a lot of times these guys are allowed to get away with this childish act.

Recently I was at a table when the dealer took his break and was replaced by one of these speed freaks. I mean this guy was like lightning. One of the ladies at the table asked him to slow down and the others grumbled out loud. He ignored their protests.

On the seventh or eighth hand that he dealt me, I got a

six/six vs. his up-card of four, a definite split move. Now he was mine!

He pointed his finger at my hand, waiting for a decision. I hesitated as though trying to think what my next move would be.

"Sir, would you make your move!" he demanded.

I looked at at him and went into a three minute oration of how this was my first time in the casino: I didn't understand the game; what were my options; I couldn't see the cards; could he count them for me; could I have change; what was the difference between splitting or doubling; what value was the ace; that I was from a little town in Idaho called Jackblack, and oddly enough we didn't play Blackjack. I did it in a very friendly nice way, but he got the point. Finally I placed a chip on the table and told him I'd like to split. He banged my first six with a four, a sure pop double down and a good excuse to go into another act.

The other players knew what was happening and were roaring at him. He was absolutely livid.

I never raised my voice, but took at the very least 5 minutes, to get in every comment and question that even remotely pertained to the game of Blackjack.

Mercifully, we came to the end of the hand. By that time he had taken more then his share of ridicule from the rest of the table. He completed the moves of the other players, in a marked reduction in speed.

The next few hands were dealt slowly and with a deadly silence between players and dealer, but you knew he was seething.

Through all of this, I noticed that the floor person observed the whole thing from a distance, but did not come over. That could have been because no loud exchanges were made, or it could have been that he knew that what was happening was the dealers own fault.

Anyhow, the regular dealer returned and the speed freak made his move to leave. He looked at me long and hard, but said nothing. However, there was no question he got the message. I haven't seen him since.

You should be quick enough to handle any of these fast dealers, but that's not the point. There are many things that you need to do in card counting, so it's nice to play at a slow, controlled game.

Don't chart tables where the dealer is one of those show-offs and don't play there.

But if the time comes when you do get stuck with one, handle it in a nice smooth manner — not nasty.

Don't be intimated by these guys and that'll be covered in an upcoming chapter.

124

HOW ABOUT LUCK?

One of the most over-used and least understood terms in the world of gambling, is that word luck. I don't know how it started, but many people seem to think luck has something to do with gambling. Here are some comments:

    a) Good luck at the races,
    b) I hope I have good luck at the crap table,
    c) Wish me luck,
    d) I'm a lucky person in gambling,
    e) I don't know how to play, but I'm lucky,
    f) Did you have any luck today?

Ever hear any of those statements? Of course you have. Many of you probably have recited them to yourself or somebody else.

Luck has no place in gambling. Either you're a perfect player and have a 50-50 chance of winning, or you're a dope, that thinks luck is gonna carry you through.

Igott Luck is a craps player, or so he thinks. He couldn't tell a bet behind the Pass Line in craps, from a crappy pass behind the line in football.

When he wins, he proclaims to the world that he was 'lucky.' When he loses, his cry is that he had bad luck. It was all in the Trend at that table. When he was in a hot Trend, a good Money Management method could kick him off some good profits.

When he was in a bad run, his Loss Limit would cut his losses. It would have absolutely nothing to do with luck. Get outa the idea that luck can help you in gambling. Only the Big 4 can help you. And you can help yourself by learning the Big 4.

My idea of good luck would be to have Dolly Parton sit at a Blackjack game across from me!

My idea of bad luck would be that her husband would be with her!

125

SPLITTING FIVES

If you absorbed the basic strategy chart that is in front of this book, you'd see that many of my moves differ from what has been handed down to us thru the years. This includes:

a) Do not always split aces,
b) Do not double 10 or 11 vs dealers 2,
c) Do not split eights or aces across the board.

Now we come to another change that I did not put in the basic strategy chart and kept it until the very end, before making my feelings known. It will be a move that is based strictly on the feelings you yourself might have for this variation.

It concerns splitting fives. We all know that when you are dealt two fives (10), you automatically double down. That move has never been challenged.

We also know that the reason we double down and split is to get more money against the dealer when he is in trouble. And there-in lies the Theory of my variation.

If you were betting five dollars and were dealt 5/5 vs the dealers 6, you could slide another chip on the table, have ten dollars in action, and wait for your double down card.

However, if you were to split those fives, you'd still have ten dollars in action, but look at the added possibilities of getting more money against that dealer when he is in trouble.

By splitting, you will receive a card on that first five. If it is a six, five, four, three or ace, you could now double down. That gives you five out of thirteen chances of getting a double down shot and being able to put another $5 against him. Same is true when the dealer gets to that second five.

Now you have a chance to put $20 against that dealer, when he is weak.

This changeover in my play has been made during the past two years and I have found it to be quite effective. Naturally you're not going to win every time, but the Theory works out the same way.

You'll never bust against his breaking hand and you'll get the chance to put more money in play at the proper time.

If you decide to make this change-over, the splits would occur against the dealers up-card of 4, 5, 6.

In a nutshell, you have two fives and dealer has:

    a) 2 . . . . you hit,
    b) 3 . . . . you double down,
    c) 4-5-6 . . . . you split,
    d) 7 . . . . you double down,
    e) 8 thru ace . . . . you hit.

You may think this move is a little way out. That's one of the reasons I held off giving it to you, so that you'll get an idea of my overall Theory, which has me playing very, very conservative when that dealer has power cards as his up-card. Then when he is in trouble, I like to go for the jugular.

This is a good move and I use it all the time. My suggestion to you would be to do it. Don't say no, until you take a long hard look at this play.

126

ENTERING A CASINO

Let's put into order the things you need to enter a casino, with an idea of card counting at a Blackjack table.

We'll assume you have absorbed everything I shot out at you through these pages and now you're gonna give it your best shot. Be sure you have all of the following:

- a) Bankroll, at least $450 for 3 Sessions at a $5 table,
- b) Be able to count one deck in 13 seconds,
- c) Be able to count six decks in 90 seconds maximum,
- d) Have 'Series' bets predetermined,
- e) Know at what point you'll insert 'soft increases,'
- f) Know how to back-count,
- g) Know how to keep side count of aces,
- h) Have decided upon method of counting,
  - 1) Single Card Method,
  - 2) Three Card Offset.
- i) Have established Win Goal — based on Bankroll,
- j) Have established Loss Limit — based on Bankroll.

That's what you need to have as you enter the field of battle. If you don't have every one of these items, you ain't ready.

And I don't mean you just have to have an idea of what they are. You gotta have your game plan down to a science. But most of all you must have your disciplined percentages etched deeply in your mind and follow them through.

Even having all of these things will not guarantee a winning day. All they do is give you a 50-50 shot.

The rest is up to you.

127

ETIQUETTE

I haven't suddenly swung over to trying to teach you how to curtsy or bow from the waist. Some of you haven't seen your shoes in years and asking you to make a bend at the waist would only open up a sewing job for your wives. Not to mention the split in the rear of your pants, that is already bucking hugh odds, trying to stay in one piece.

Etiquette goes a little deeper. It's how you conduct yourself at a table. You've all seen our friend I. M. Loud and immediately struck up an instant dislike.

Same goes for some little irritating things you might do at a table. Things your wife puts up with, cause she's stuck with you, but things that could irritate strangers:

a) Smoking.

b) Drinking too much and becoming a bore,

c) Talking too much,

    1) The other players may not be interested in your run of good hands, or where you're from, or how successful you are.

d) Trying to be too friendly with the dealer,

    1) Some people make real pests of themselves, trying hard to make small talk.

e) Stop grumbling when you're losing,

f) Don't gloat when you're in a hot run,

g) Don't beg for comps,

h) Don't offer suggestions on how to play to the other patrons.

It's funny, but a real pest stands out like a sore thumb at

a table. The other people are wrapped up in their own thoughts and maybe aren't interested in your weak attempt to be the funny man at that table.

A classy person stands out. Funny part is that the quieter you act, the more people tend to notice you.

The casino people are more apt to reward the sharp player with comps, etc. Etiquette at a table is a small part of your day, but it'll make you feel like a big person.

128

COMPS

I don't enjoy writing a chapter on Comps, yet it is a big part of the casino scene, so I gotta touch on it.

Naturally it's taken from the word complimentary and it comes in the form of a gift that the casinos want to give to certain players.

It just so happens that those certain players are the ones who bet the most money. It's a status type thing, which has been blown completely out of it's original intent.

Comps started back in Vegas many years ago, when the casinos offered free drinks to it's patrons. It's a nice move, to get players to stay at that particular casino and play. Nothing wrong with that.

Then the casinos started giving rooms, show tickets and meals to their preferred playes (high rollers), and the dam was broken. Every guy who enters a casino thinks that he deserves to be 'comped,' because of the action he gives the house.

Dick de Dorke is a dork of the highest order. He enters the casino with seventy two dollars and eighty six cents in his jeans. Blackjack is his game and he slides onto one of the stools.

Within ten minutes he has confirmed the fact that he is a jerk. He buys in for twenty dollars and bets $5 a pop.

His first words to the dealer are: "Can I have a waitress please." He knows that the casinos offer free drinks to everyone, regardless of the amount of their bets.

As per usual, a floor person will come over to the table

311

to check things out and maybe say hello to a player he recognizes. Our hero Dick de Dorke, finishing off his double scotch and soda, addresses the floor person: "Hey Mac, what's the chance of getting a meal, or even a bite to eat at the deli?"

Naturally the floor person knows Dorky has only been at the tables for a few hands. In a nice way he'll explain that they must chart his play, to get a line on his action.

Dick de Dorke goes into an oration about taking his play elsewhere and all the usual garbage.

Get one thing straight about comps. Getting a few drinks or cocktails at the tables, is a tremendously generous move on the part of the casinos.

The comps belong to the house. Let them choose whomever they wish to give them to. If you warrant it, you'll get it. But don't be a jerk and beg for something you really don't deserve.

Usually the house requires approximately 3 or 4 hours of play, at a certain level, to give a comp. Following is only a rough idea of what a certain house might have as their guideline:

    a) Weekday: 3 hours at average of $10 per hand...Deli,

    b) Weeknight: 3-4 hours at average of $10 per hand...Deli or show,

    c) Weekdays: 3-4 hours at average of $25 per hand...show or meal,

    d) Weeknights: 3-4 hours at average of $25 per hand...show, meal, rooms,

    e) Weekends: 3-4 hours at average of $20 per hand...Deli,

    f) Weekend nights: 3-4 hours at average of $50 per hand...show, meals, rooms,

g) High roller...Red carpet treatment.

You will also find times during the week, and in the winter time, when $5 average hand gets you taken care of. It is strictly dependant on how long you play, for what amount and the time of the week. The slower the period, the better chance you have of getting a comp.

But please get that nonsense out of your head that the casinos owe you comps, cause they don't. They're controlled as to what they can give out and have the right to limit these gifts to the people they choose to bestow them on.

Dick de Dorke oughta be happy he gets a free cocktail for his play. You enter a casino to win money from them. Now you want them to feed and house you, too. You got some set of nerves.

This thing on comps is blown out of proportion. Become a perfect player, Learn How to Win, pick up your profits and go buy your own meal. It'll taste just as good.

129

TIPPING

A touchy subject, but one of the most misunderstood moves in the casino. I get deluged with questions on this matter at every lecture and you gotta read between the lines, to catch the full impact of what I'm saying regarding this subject.

Tipping is done for a purpose, to reward a person for a service. It is natural to tip a girl in a restaurant when she has served your meal, or when a mechanic does an extra nice job on your car.

In the casinos, the dealers work for a tad above minimum wage and rely on tips to bring home a decent pay. If you think they're not aware of your tips, you're wrong.

If you play at a table and tip a particular dealer, you'll notice when he goes on a break that he'll alert the replacement dealer, as to who is tipping.

He'll point you out in a nice way and say: "Take care of my friend." He is telling that new dealer that you are putting money in play for the dealers and the new guy will usually be extra friendly to you. This way they hope that it'll wake up the other patrons at the table and get them to start kicking in.

I tip for a purpose. Usually a dealer keeps a sharp lookout on your hand, to make sure he doesn't make a mistake and miscount your pay-offs. He'll remind you of double down situations and make sure your glass is never empty.

In fact, sometimes he is so anxious to please you, that he gets down-right sloppy and pays you too much for a winning hand, or forgets to take a bet when you lose.

I usually feel sorry for the dealer when I see him mistakenly pay me $23 for a $17 wager. Since I don't want to embarrass him, by calling his mistake to the attention of everyone else, I give him a message some other way. I'll put a chip in play for him on the next hand. Funny, a lot of times he continues his sloppy overpayments, but that's another story...

You tip by putting a chip in front of your bet on the table and that means the dealer is playing with you. Suppose you're betting $10 and put $1 out for the dealer and a double down moves comes up. Put your $10 up and $1 for him. Now he is going to win twice as much. You've got his attention when you place a chip with your hand.

Don't just give him the tip — put it in play for him. They like the idea of the action and naturally the chance to win twice as much.

There's also a time to tip. I usually wait until I'm ahead, before starting to tip the dealer. Do the same thing. You know you'll be at that table awhile and he'll have a chance to get 'sloppy.'

If you're losing, there's no reason to tip, as you may be gone shortly. Also, I've seen people tip when they leave a table. Can't see that move. Tip as you go along and see what happens. It's obvious nothing can happen if you're no longer at that table.

I am not intimating that dealers cheat, it's just that some get a little sloppier than others, during long dealing days.

Question: Should I tip?

Answer: Yes.

Question: How often?

Answer: As you're winning, a dollar every 6-7
         hands.
Question: Should I tip if I'm losing?
Answer: No.
Question: Should I leave a tip when I leave a table?
Answer: No.
Question: Why am I tipping?
Answer: For nice service.
Question: If dealer doesn't get sloppy after 5 or 6
         tips, should I continue?
Answer: If Dolly Parton stopped returning my
         phone calls, I'd still love her, but I
         wouldn't call her again.

Tipping is an art, just like playing the harp. You gotta
know how to manipulate the instrument.

130

INTIMIDATION

This is something that plagues people in all walks of life. They are constantly intimidated by something or other.

In the casinos, people are intimidated by the whole atmosphere — because it's new to them and they don't fully know how to handle it.

A dealer in a white shirt and black tie, having just completed a three month course in dealing, has a little cockiness about him. A patron sitting at his table may inadvertently touch his chips, after he has placed his bet on the table.

This is a no-no in Atlantic City. You cannot touch your chips or your cards. All of a sudden this wise apple dealer may say: "Sir, you're not supposed to touch your chips, one more time and I'll have to ask you to leave the table."

The poor guy turns eight shades of orange, purple and pink. On the outside, he'd put the mouth in his place. In the casino, he is in a new world and can't handle it.

If you're at a table with a nasty dealer, there's nothing wrong with reporting him to the floor person. The majority of these dealers are very congenial, but you'll get the bad apples and they have no right talking down to you.

My buddy in Las Vegas, Howie Goldstein, is one of the sharpest players I have ever seen. He's a counter in Blackjack and goes to the tables with a decent amount of money.

Once he was at a table, where the dealer made a glaring mistake on the hand of the player sitting next to him. The dealer had 18 and the player had a six card hand of 19. When the hand was completed, the dealer took the guy's bet. The player looked at Howie, but didn't say a word to the dealer.

Howie told the guy to speak up — that he won the hand. You know what the player replied? "I'm afraid to...he might get mad."

Can you imagine? The dealer took his money and he is scared to say anything. If a guy put his hand in your pocket on the street and pulled out your change, there'd be a riot. In the casino a guy turns to jelly, when confronted with a similar situation.

Anyhow, about an hour later, the same thing happened to Howie and he calmly told the dealer: "I think you made a mistake — I won that hand."

The dealer ignored him. Howie said it again: "Dealer...you made a mistake with that last hand. I won and you took my money."

The dealer sneered at him and started to deal the next hand. Howie stood up and placed a hand on the dealers wrist and in a very calm way declared: "Sonny, back up those cards or I'll break your wrist."

A quick note about Howie. He was a star athlete growing up in the friendly confines of Jersey City, NJ. If you have played basketball on the streets of Jersey City as a teenager, you know of what I speak. You fear nothing!

A floor person rushed to the table and Howie calmly explained the matter. The cards were backed up and Howie was reimbursed his money, plus his winnings. This is not a story, it is a fact. It is also not something that happens every day in the casinos.

But when you do play, do not be intimidated. There's no reason to be, if you're done nothing wrong. The casinos are not your enemy. Neither are the dealers or floor people.

Intimidation is in the minds of the players themselves. You think that it is a whole new world and you're afraid to make a mistake. The next time you're even a little bit awed by the surroundings, give Howie a call. In fifteen minutes he'll have you thinking you own the place.

131

THE ULTIMATE GOAL

We've come full cyle in the approach to Blackjack, by way of Card Counting. The system is very simple to understand and will be a strong tool in improving your basic strategy.

But I've told you that enough times already. The message should now be ingrained in your arsenal of ammunition, in which to attack the casinos.

What I want to emphasize is the reason you gamble. You know that I think anyone who gambles for fun or entertainment is a dork. There is no reason to risk your money — just for the sheer pleasure of having something going for you.

The object of gambling is to win money. It *is* the ultimate goal of all gamblers to catch the longest hot streak in the history of gambling.

It *should* be the ultimate goal of every player to just win. There is no other reason to gamble.

You already know the things that will help you to win: **LITTLE 3 & BIG 4!**

You know my **THEORY** of conservative play. I beg you to approach gambling with a **LOGICAL** outlook. When you get in a hot **TREND,** make the enemy pay.

Don't play unless you've got a decent **BANKROLL.** Be sure you're perfect in the **KNOWLEDGE OF THE GAME** you attack. Perfect my **MONEY MANAGEMENT** method.

And finally, have the almighty guts to follow the strict rules of **DISCIPLINE** that I stress, page after page after page after page.

If you tie it into your **WIN GOALS** and **LOSS LIMITS,** you'll be among the best players in the casino. If only you would realize it...

The Ultimate Goal in gambling should be to walk out of the casino a winner. Keep that thought in mind.

I hope you have learned something from these chapters on card counting and Money Management. As you become more proficient in gambling, you will add your own theories and eventually become a perfect player.

You will Learn How To Win and you will love it. And that beats losing, any old day.

Since I abhorr any reference to luck when it comes to gambling, I won't go mentioning that ill-advised approach to the games of chance.

But I would like to offer my sincere best wishes to you and your family, in anything you do. If it's worth doing — it's worth doing right. "SO YOU WANNA BE A GAMBLER!" Be the best!!!

HAPPY WINNINGS

JOHN PATRICK